MISSING THE POINT

IT'S TIME TO USHER IN A NEW GENERATION OF CHRISTIANITY

AMY SKOLL

WESTBOW
PRESS®
A DIVISION OF THOMAS NELSON
& ZONDERVAN

WestBow Press books may be ordered through booksellers or by contacting:

WestBow Press
A Division of Thomas Nelson & Zondervan
1663 Liberty Drive
Bloomington, IN 47403
www.westbowpress.com
844-714-3454

ISBN: 978-1-6642-3698-1 (sc)
ISBN: 978-1-6642-3699-8 (hc)
ISBN: 978-1-6642-3697-4 (e)

Library of Congress Control Number: 2021911614

Print information available on the last page.

WestBow Press rev. date: 07/14/2021

CONTENTS

ACKNOWLEDGMENTS

A special thanks to my husband, my parents, and my tribe of girlfriends who have provided so much love, support, feedback, and encouragement throughout this journey. I couldn't have done this without you!

CHAPTER 1
INTRODUCTION

To the world, I am many things—a professor, a wife, a new mom, a writer, a basic white girl, an extrovert, an Independent, an overachiever, a Californian, and a millennial. And as much as I strongly identify with all those things, the only thing that I should, and want to, be known for is being a Christian. Yet in today's world, particularly in the United States over the past few decades, this is by far the most controversial and least popular of all my identities. Being a Christian is neither popular nor politically correct. For many, being a Christian means being narrow-minded, judgmental, self-righteous, ignorant, racist, sexist, antigay, and a radical fundamentalist. I will be the first to admit that, unfortunately, there are Christians everywhere who are all those things. In fact, this is not the first time that Christians have created a bad name for themselves (hello, Crusades, indulgences, colonialism, slavery, etc.), and it will most certainly not be the last.

The real question becomes, What does it look like to be a Christian in a time when being a Christian is unpopular? I am in no way claiming that I am the voice of my generation, but what I can say is that as a millennial, I am watching an entire generation walk away from the church, abandoning or watering down their faith, compromising on biblical truths, and trying to overcompensate for the bad reputation Christian believers have gained. On the other extreme, I also see Christians becoming hardened, clinging to their beliefs and shoving them down the throats of anyone who will listen. Instead of channeling wisdom and discernment, there are many

Christians who do not know how to pick their battles and others who don't know how to stand up for their beliefs at all. Afraid of coming across as judgmental, many Christians don't take a stance on anything, and as a result, their faith wavers in the face of the smallest resistance to their beliefs. Others are desperate to demonstrate that they are Christians but don't know how to communicate their beliefs effectively to others. And some are not afraid to communicate their beliefs but are misguided on what the Bible actually teaches.

I am writing this book because I fundamentally believe that it is not only possible but is also our duty as believers to be effective ambassadors for Christ in a world that does not understand our beliefs, customs, convictions, and experiences. However, I am not naive to the fact that this job, although more important than ever, has become more difficult than ever. As ambassadors for Christ, we do not want to come across as insensitive to the cultures and belief systems of those around us. But at the same time, it is our job to accurately represent the gospel without succumbing to a watered-down version of Christianity in the process. Our job rests on the tension between truth and love, which is one of the most difficult balances to strike. In fact, this balance is impossible to find without the wisdom and discernment of the Holy Spirit.

As the next generation of leaders, we have the opportunity to change the reputation of Christianity in the United States and in the world. As much as we can learn from the generations above us, they are limited by their own experiences and the culture and environment that they grew up in. Research tells us that we have more access to education and are more tech savvy, connected, globally minded, and diverse than previous generations. And with these trends come important questions about politics, gender, sexuality, race, poverty, morality, activism, and the role of the church. Given the rapidly changing political and social climate, it is no wonder that Christians are having a hard time reconciling the vast amounts of information they are receiving on a daily basis with what the Bible actually teaches. In a post-truth era, with a constant influx of news rapidly infiltrating our information sources, the need for clarity is ever more apparent. Ironically, despite the high levels of education we have received and our abundant access to information, very few young people actually know what the Word of God says and how to interpret it, especially in a different cultural context. Biblical illiteracy is rampant, and as a result, the confusion surrounding what it means to be a Christian has become increasingly apparent.

In writing this book, then, I hope to inspire a generation of Christians who are not only aware of the important issues of the day but also know how to effectively talk about them as an ambassador for Christ. In doing so, I hope to remind and teach my fellow believers what the Word of God says and how to reconcile biblical truths with cultural and political trends. I wholeheartedly believe that it is possible to stick to our beliefs, not accepting a watered-down version of Christianity, without coming across as judgmental, insensitive, or rude. In fact, the Bible shows us a perfect example of how to do this through the life of Jesus Christ Himself. Jesus was often controversial and unpopular and went to the cross and died for His beliefs. However, Jesus was known for His compassion, grace, kindness, and love. Even those who killed Him could find no fault with Him. Like Jesus, as Christians, we should strive to be blameless and unashamed in a world that wants to place blame and shame. We need to do better and be better, not because our salvation depends on it but because we are doing a disservice to an entire generation who is lost and confused, desperately seeking truth, and unsure of what to look for or how to identify truth when they find it. I hope that in reading this, your faith is refreshed, your love for God is amplified, your hope is restored, and you feel empowered to take on the mission of Christ in a world that is increasingly in opposition to Christianity and what it stands for.

A brief note on what this book is and what this book is not:

1. Although I am a millennial writing from the perspective of a millennial, this book is not just targeted toward millennials. I believe that all generations of Christians need to hear this message, and the issues brought up in this book are not just questions in the minds of millennials; they are questions in the minds all believers living in the world today. So don't let my Harry Potter and pop culture references deter you from reading this book! As believers, we are all one in Jesus Christ, so I think it is important for us to all be on the same page. Christ's reputation here on earth is shaped

not just by a handful of believers but by the entire body of Christ. Therefore, my intention with this book is to start a dialogue among believers of all different ages about how Christ could be better proclaimed in this rapidly shifting world.

2. My primary goal with this book is to create an attitude shift among believers. Therefore, I am looking at the big picture here, and I do not want to get bogged down by the minutiae of any particular issue; I want to get at the heart of the issue, not the issue itself. There are many books and resources out there that address in more detail every topic that I bring up in this book. However, I don't want to just parrot the arguments and resources that are already out there. Instead, I want to take a step back, pull out a wider lens, and ask the bigger questions that are being neglected. I do not claim to be an expert on any issue brought up in this book. I am, however, a devoted follower of Christ who desires for the gospel to be proclaimed and for Christ's love to be magnified in this world. I am not trying to spark controversy or advocate for a particular set of policies, ideologies, or political parties but rather to get us all to think about the areas where we are perhaps missing the point. I want us to think critically about the messages we are proclaiming, asking ourselves whether they are of this world or from our heavenly Father.

CHAPTER 2
WHO IS GOD?

May we never lose our wonder
May we never lose our wonder
Wide eyed and mystified
May we be just like a child
Staring at the beauty of our King.

—"Wonder" by Bethel Music and Amanda Cook

There were many ways I could have started this book, and I toyed with many different ideas. However, when it came down to it, I kept coming back to this idea that as a society we have lost our understanding of who God is. We are so preoccupied with what is wrong with the world, what is wrong with the church, what is wrong with the Bible, and what is wrong with politics that we have turned our attention to finding worldly solutions for eternal problems, taking our eyes off God in the process. Although we often have noble intentions, we get so caught up in what's trending and so engrossed in conversations that are hot right now that we often forget to take a step back and look at the big picture.

For example, young people today care a lot about politics and social justice. Inequality makes our blood boil. We are resistant to patterns of authority and the status quo. We see the world how it could be and want to be a part of the change. And these are all noble, holy goals. In fact, Romans 8:19–23 (ESV) states this:

For the creation waits with eager longing for the revealing of the children of God; for the creation was subjected to futility, not of its own will but by the will of the one who subjected it, in hope that the creation itself will be set free from its bondage to decay and will obtain the freedom of the glory of the children of God. We know that the whole creation has been groaning in labor pains until now; and not only the creation, but we ourselves, who have the first fruits of the Spirit, groan inwardly while we wait for adoption, the redemption of our bodies.

I love this verse because I think it captures what so many of us feel but don't know how to express. There is a deep dissatisfaction with the way things are and a collective longing for things to be restored. The world is afflicted with brokenness, and we want something to be done about it. In the New Testament, the word *groaning* is used as an expression for mental distress, of deep sorrow and of woe. Deep down, at the core of our beings, we know that the world is not right, that it is broken and in need of repair. We feel a longing for the world to be redeemed, to see justice, to see wrongs made right, to see people delivered from their bondage, to see hope restored, to see peace on earth.

I don't know about you, but sometimes I feel physical pain when I think about how broken our world is. Sometimes I have to cut myself off from the news because it can cause me so much anxiety and frustration. These feelings are often amplified by the fact that I have a PhD in political science with an emphasis in international relations, which means sometimes I can't escape thinking about the world and all its shortcomings because it is my job to stay informed. The more I learn about the world, the more hopeless I sometimes feel because there is so much that needs to be done—and how can I, as one individual, fix any of it?

I know that I am not alone in this. A recent study conducted by a political scientist out of the University of Nebraska, Lincoln found that around 40 percent of people stated that politics was a cause of stress in their lives, with 20 percent claiming that they had lost sleep and had felt depressed due to politics.[1] In addition, between 10 and 30 percent of respondents admitted that politics had caused them to feel anger, frustration, hate, or guilt or had caused them to say something they later regretted.[2] Another 20 percent said that politics had affected their friendships.[3]

So, why is politics so divisive and such a cause of anxiety in our lives? Because deep down we want the world to be a better place, but we all have different solutions for how to get there. We care deeply about the state of society and are fearful of others who might compromise the well-being of ourselves and our communities. We long for things to be made right and are desperate for some sort of solution.

Here is the problem though. Our solutions for all the world's problems are also of this world, which means they are imperfect. They will consistently fall short of our expectations and will not satisfy. We have embarked on this endless pursuit of trying to make the world a better place, forgetting that the reason God had to send His Son to die on the cross is because we cannot do it on our own. Our goals may be noble, our efforts admirable, but without God, we cannot restore this world. We may debate the merits of different policies, advocate for new programs and institutions, campaign for new leaders and ideas, and champion new causes, but at the end of the day, the world will continue to be broken until Jesus returns.

I do not say this to be a Debbie Downer or to discourage all the passion and activism that Christians can contribute. I will talk more in future chapters about the importance of believers taking up social justice causes and engaging in activist efforts. However, as Christians, if we continue to cling to earthly solutions and proselytize a redemption plan for the world in which God is not at the center, then we are preaching a false gospel. In other words, we are taking God out of Christianity. As the verses above in Romans emphasize, although all creation groans for the redemption of our broken world, our hope is not in an earthly redemption but in a spiritual redemption. We eagerly await the day when we will all be reunited with

---

[1] Rhitu Chatterjee, "Stressed Out by Politics? Here's How to Keep Caring without Losing Your Cool," *NPR*, September 25, 2019, https://www.npr.org/sections/health-shots/2019/09/25/764216567/is-politics-stressing-you-out-heres-how-to-keep-caring-without-losing-your-cool.

[2] Chatterjee, "Stressed Out By Politics?"

[3] Chatterjee, "Stressed Out By Politics?"

Christ, as His sons and daughters, reveling in the glory of God. Our hope is not in a patched-up, bandaged version of this world but in the day when God restores heaven on earth, making all things new.

Therefore, before we jump into all these important issues that are facing our world and the church today, I felt called to reiterate that we serve a big, almighty God who reigns above all creation—to remind ourselves of who God is and why we, as individuals, and as a global society are in need of a savior. If we lived in a perfect world, or a world that could be perfected by the human race, we would not need God. Each shortcoming that we come across in ourselves, in society, in the church, in politics, and in the world is a glaring reminder that we cannot do this on our own without God. Each shortcoming is an opportunity to praise the one who has the whole world in His hands, the one who is before all things and holds all things together, the Alpha and the Omega, the Great I Am, our Everlasting God.

The problem is, for most of us, we don't really understand or know who God is. Even though we have been invited into a personal relationship with God, He often seems distant, or we are unsure of how to foster a connection with Him. As a result, we often spend most of our lives operating under false assumptions about His character and His role and purpose in our lives. Many of us never actually take the time to get to know Him, out of fear, uncertainty, or even sometimes laziness. We talk about God as an abstract mythical character rather than someone we know and love deeply on a personal level.

Let me ask you a question. Have you ever been misunderstood? Have you ever had someone question your motives or character without giving you the benefit of the doubt? Have you ever had someone jump to conclusions about you without taking the time to hear the backstory or why you did what you did? The reality is we, unfortunately, live in an imperfect world where people do not have a perfect understanding of all things at all times. As a result, it is inevitable that at times we will jump to conclusions, cast judgment prematurely, and interpret situations incorrectly without knowing the full picture. We are only human.

Imagine then how much we, as imperfect human beings, must misunderstand God. We make false judgments with people and situations here on earth all the time; therefore, how in the world are we to fully understand the eternal big picture? We are bound by time and space and have a limited capacity to perceive things beyond ourselves. Most of the time, we don't even fully understand ourselves, let alone how everything in the world fits together in one big masterpiece.

And yet, despite our limitations, we are quick to judge God and jump to conclusions about His intentions. When things don't make sense, it is our natural inclination to point the finger at God, rather than to admit that maybe we don't have the full picture. It is not our nature to give God the benefit of the doubt. We tend to view things only from our perspective, and from where we are standing, things don't make a ton of sense. Why would God do things this way? Didn't He realize that humans were going to mess everything up? Why doesn't God just step in and fix everything? Does God just have a sick sense of humor?

Fortunately for us, God isn't some emo teenager writing song lyrics about how hard it is to be so misunderstood all the time. However, He does call us to trust Him, even when things don't make sense. Proverbs 3:5 calls us to "Trust in the LORD with all your heart and lean not on your own understanding." In other words, when things don't make sense, trust that God is working in ways beyond our comprehension, instead of drawing conclusions from what we think we know.

For example, for those of you Harry Potter fans out there, think about Professor Snape. Most of us hated him for most of the series and never understood until the end why Dumbledore continued to trust Snape despite all of what seemed to be red flags. Snape appeared to be despicable and dangerous, but once you came to understand his backstory, everything started to make more sense. Once Snape's true character had been revealed, it became clear that all our judgments about him throughout the series were unwarranted. Dumbledore's unfailing trust in Snape no longer seemed irrational but intentional and justified.

God is, of course, on a whole different level than Professor Snape, but this analogy is still useful. When we have a correct understanding of God's character and intentions, we are going to trust Him even in seasons that might seem complicated or confusing to an outsider. People might think we are crazy sometimes to put our trust in God when the world is falling apart, but we understand the bigger picture and know that God has a reason for everything, even when things don't make sense. Romans 8:28

says, "And we know that in all things God works for the good of those who love him, who have been called according to his purpose." Do you truly believe that God is working for your good? When times get rough, when things don't make sense, is it your natural instinct to believe that God has a plan? Or are you quick to jump to conclusions, assuming God is cruel, heartless, and maniacal? If God is the same, yesterday, today, and forever, why do our opinions of God change? The issue isn't that God changes; it's that we are fickle people who are easily manipulated by our emotions and circumstances, and it is easier to blame God rather than own up to the mess we have all gotten ourselves in.

COMPREHENDING A MIND-BLOWING GOD

I think one of the biggest reasons people have an incorrect view of God is because our human brains are unable to fully comprehend the perfect duality of many of God's attributes. God is perfectly merciful but perfectly just. He is in this moment, but He is also outside of time. He is all-knowing and all-powerful, but He lets us act in accordance with our own free will. Unable to grasp how God's attributes work together in perfect harmony, we tend to focus on some of His attiributes and neglect others.

For example, some believers proclaim a message of love and acceptance, minimizing sin and failing to talk about the importance of repentance and God's forgiveness. This is the "Jesus is your homeboy" model. Others preach a message of fire and brimstone, damning people to hell for their sins, forgetting that God is love and that Jesus didn't come to judge the world but to save the world (John 12:47).

In order to be a follower of Christ, you have to get comfortable with the tension. As much as we would like to be able to put God into neat little boxes, the God we serve does not fit in a box. And thank goodness for that! God is not like the genie in Aladdin who is contained by a magic lamp, who must follow a strict set of rules and must show up whenever He is beckoned to respond to our requests. Although I am sure we could all come up with three wishes we would love God to answer right now, we do not want our God, the Creator of the universe, to be reduced to the limited and constrained power of a genie.

A genie can only do what a human can think up. Its power is only as big as the human imagination. One of the major points of the movie

Aladdin is that what we wish for is not always as good as it seems. We may think that wishing for money or status will make everything better, but those things will not satisfy the eternal desires of our hearts. Even if we were altruistic with our wishes and wished for things like world peace, there are still so many questions to be answered. What does world peace look like? Who's definition of world peace? Can world peace be sustained on its own? Does world peace require justice? If so, who must face the consequences? If we truly do achieve world peace, then what? Will people just mess things up again, or do people have to be made perfect in order to keep the peace? Then should you wish for people to be perfect instead? If so, what does perfect mean? Would everyone be the same if they were all perfect? Would things be boring if everyone was the same?

I know that was a lot of questions, but that was kind of the point. These are all questions that cannot be fully answered by a human being. The smartest, wisest, most well-read, most well-educated, most experienced individuals throughout history have consistently sought to solve the world's problems but to no avail. If human beings were able to save the world, we would have done so by now.

That is why we need a God who is bigger than the human mind can comprehend—a God who can hold all time and space in His thoughts without His mind exploding, a God who can see the big picture but can also give each detail attention and care. That is the type of God I want to serve.

The difficulty in serving a God who is bigger than we can comprehend is that we sometimes have to accept that we won't always understand everything. In Jeremiah 55:8, it states, "For my thoughts are not your thoughts, neither are your ways my ways, declares the Lord. For as the heavens are higher than the earth, so are my ways higher than your ways and my thoughts than your thoughts." Are you willing to submit to the fact that God's plan is outside the realm of our own understanding? When asked about God's purpose for our lives or this world, are you willing to say, "I don't know, but I am confident that God knows better than I do, and I trust Him to make the right call."

Whereas the controlling side of me is hesitant to give up the reins, stubbornly holding on to the belief that I can do things on my own, there is another part of me that finds relief in the fact that I don't have to figure all things out. It is not my responsibility to save the world and to fix all the world's problems. It is OK that I don't have all the answers. There is comfort in knowing that even when the world doesn't make sense, I serve a God who will one day make sense of everything.

As much as we hate to admit it, when we don't know where we are going or what we are doing, it is a relief when we finally give up the reins to someone who does. The problem is we first have to come to the realization that we don't know where we are going or what we are doing. No one likes to admit that they need help, but when it comes to saving the world, we need *a lot* of help! We are out of our league. We can keep trying to fill the God-sized hole in the world with our temporary earthy solutions, or we can take a step back, throw up our hands, and tell God that we need His help. And when we finally do that, we can begin to see the ways that God is working in this world.

In many ways, it is like sitting back and watching a world-class chef make you a surprise dinner. You don't know what the end result will be, and you don't know how they are going to make it. They may even use new techniques that you have never seen before or use ingredients you have never heard of. They may pair things together that you never thought would go together. However, as delicious scents waft from the kitchen, your mouth starts to water, and you think, *Wow, this is going to be good*. The chef knows what they are doing, and you trust that the end result will be better than anything you could have cooked up in the kitchen.

MAY WE NEVER LOSE OUR WONDER

The question then becomes, If God doesn't need our help, why does He even let us try? We can trust that at the end of the day, God has it all figured out and is going to take care of everything; however, we are still here on this earth facing real issues. Is it even worth our time to do anything, or should we tap out and just wait for the end of the world? Why would God entrust us with the world if He knows we aren't capable of making it right?

Here is an analogy I heard several years ago that has stuck with me ever since. One day, this dad was out washing his car and was almost done cleaning up when his two-year-old son came outside and asked if he could help. Although the dad was wrapping things up and was almost finished, he saw how excited his son was and decided to let him "help." Delighted by the opportunity to work with his dad, the little boy went and picked up a leaf and started using the leaf to "wash" the car. The father's heart was touched. Although the son was clearly not making a huge difference in the cleanliness of the car, the important thing was that his son wanted to spend time with his dad and was eager to help.

If you haven't guessed it already, God is the dad in this story, and we are the two-year-old boy. When we love our dad, we want to spend time with him, and we care about the things that he cares about (in this case, the car). We even want to be helpful and useful to him, even though our efforts are as miniscule as the leaf wiping down the car. The dad didn't need his son's help with the car, but he let him help because he loved his son, wanted to spend time with him, and wanted to honor the fact that his son was eager to help. The car would never get fully washed if the little boy was left to clean the car on his own with just his small leaf, but together with his dad, the car will eventually get clean.

Analogously, God doesn't need our help when it comes to fixing and saving the world. We may become impatient and start trying to fix things on our own, but without God, our efforts are meaningless and aren't even going to make a dent. Nevertheless, our heavenly Father loves us so much that He is touched by our willingness to help and our desire to be part of the process. He wants to spend time with us and wants to honor our eagerness to help. He even knows that allowing us to help out will build our character and our intimacy with Him. Therefore, He allows us to partner with Him on His plan to save the world, knowing that the process might take longer but is important for our edification. He doesn't need us, but He chooses to use us.

To reiterate, God is not a genie that we just call upon to do our bidding. Our goal is not to figure out how to fix the world on our own and then ask God for help to enact our plans. God isn't just our sponsor or our financial backer. He isn't just sitting on the sidelines waiting for us to call Him into the game. He isn't just sitting back, wringing His hands, hoping we figure it all out in time. It is not like God is just waiting for our Christmas list, hoping that world peace will be on it.

He is alive and active and has set a plan in motion before the beginning of time. He invites us into His plan and allows us to opt in, to be a part of

His mission, even though He doesn't actually need our help. He then takes our little leaves that we offer up to contribute and multiplies the effort so that the entire car gets washed.

It's just like the little boy who offers up five loaves and two fishes that Jesus uses to feed five thousand. Jesus could have easily fed the five thousand without those five loaves and two fishes, but He chose to use them to honor the little boy's generosity. Think of how excited that little boy must have been, knowing that Jesus used *his* loaves and fish to feed five thousand! Think of how that little boy's faith must have increased watching Jesus partner with him to do a miracle. God doesn't need us to do miracles, but if He can partner with us to do a miracle so that our faith might also increase in the process, then that is a beautiful thing.

As you proceed through the rest of this book, I want you to keep in mind that the heavenly Father we serve is a big God, far beyond our comprehension. In response, our goal should be to strive to have the heart of a little child who loves their dad so much that they love the things he loves; they want to do the things he does; they want to partner with their dad in exciting projects, learning from him in the process. When the little child doesn't understand something, they ask their dad why and sit at his feet to take in what their dad has to say. They trust their dad and know that their dad has their best interests at heart. They don't question his motives or act like they know better but look up at their dad with admiration and wonder. They want to be like their dad.

Do you want to be like your heavenly Father? Do you love the things your heavenly Father loves? Do you want to sit at the feet of your heavenly Father to ask questions and learn how and why the world is the way it is? Do you want to partner with your heavenly Father on cool projects and learn from Him in the process? Do you look up to your heavenly Father with admiration and wonder?

Or are you more like a teenager who is always questioning their parents' motives, convinced their parents are out to get them, to ruin their life? Are you quick to jump to conclusions without knowing the full picture? Do you see your heavenly Father just as a credit card, there to bail you out when you need it, or to get you flashy stuff that deep down you don't really need? Are you always complaining about how God is misunderstanding you or your needs, instead of wondering how you may be misunderstanding God? Are you worried that your heavenly Father might ruin your street cred, making you seem weird or politically incorrect in front of your friends? Are you quick to assume that your heavenly Father is just out of date or out of step with the times, rather than trusting that some wisdom supersedes all time and space?

This is why Jesus said in Matthew 18:3, "Unless you change and become like little children, you will never enter the kingdom of heaven." The more we lose our wonder, the more we forget our humility in relation to God. We start to think we know better, becoming critical and forgetting what is truly important.

Therefore, before you proceed with the rest of this book, I encourage you to examine your heart and ask yourself whether you have let yourself become hardened by the world. Is cynicism your first instinct? Are you willing to throw your heavenly Father under the bus for the sake of arguments and perspectives that are trending right now? Are you more prone to ask how God fits into your beliefs about the world, rather than asking how your beliefs about the world should be shaped by your belief and faith and God? Do you keep the big picture in mind, knowing that we serve a God who is beyond our understanding, or are you constantly missing the point by clinging to worldly arguments that are only half-rooted in truth?

CHAPTER 3
THE PLAGUE OF BIBLICAL ILLITERACY

Oh, to grace how great a debtor
daily I'm constrained to be!
Let thy goodness like a fetter
Bind my wandering heart to Thee
Prone to wander, Lord, I feel it
Prone to leave the God I love
Here's my heart, oh, take and seal it
Seal it for Thy courts above.

—"Come Thou Fount" by Kings Kaleidoscope

With the previous chapter, I started with the importance of knowing and trusting God. If we don't have a correct view of God in our lives, how can we even proceed? There are so many things that we want to change about the church and the world, but without God at the center of it all, all our efforts are meaningless. Instead of treating God like a genie that we summon when we have a request or complaint, we should be striving to have a heart of a child who knows that their dad has their back no matter what and wants good things for his children. Even though God doesn't need our help, He allows us to partner with Him in His holy mission for creation if we learn to trust Him and His character.

However, if we are going to trust God and His redemption plan for our lives and all creation, we also have to decide whether or not we also trust His

Word (a.k.a. the Bible). Second Timothy 3:16–17 states, "All Scripture is God-breathed and is useful for teaching, rebuking, correcting and training in righteousness so that the servant of God may be thoroughly equipped for every good work." Here Timothy is claiming that God breathed His life into scripture just like He breathed life into Adam (Genesis 2:7). The Bible is thus an extension of God, and as John 1:1 states, "In the beginning was the Word, and the Word was with God, and the Word was God." In other words, the Bible cannot be separated from God. God is His Word, and His Word is God.

Hebrews 4:12 also says that "the word of God is alive and active." God's Word is not just some dead book that only relates to a specific time in history. The beauty of God's Word is that it is just as relevant today as it was two thousand years ago. It is still moving and working in the lives of people today. God is not dead, and neither is His Word. It is still useful for teaching, rebuking, correcting, and training in righteousness. Today, it is still equipping the servant of God for every good work.

The problem is we live in an era in which many people would say that they still trust God, but they would also say that they do not trust the Bible. Even though the Bible says that God and His Word are the same thing, we have dichotomized them. We have somehow deemed it acceptable to believe in one without the other.

Imagine receiving a love letter from your significant other in the mail. In the era of DMs and text messages, snail mail may be difficult for some of you to wrap your head around, but I am guessing that most of you would see this as a romantic gesture and would love to receive a love letter from someone you love. The fact that they took the time to write out how they felt about you and wanted to do something intentional that conveyed how much you mean to them would be incredibly meaningful.

What if, however, upon receiving the letter, your first thoughts were to question the legitimacy of the letter? How do you know that the letter is actually from your significant other? How can you trust whether what was written is meaningful and true? What if they were lying about their feelings? How do you know if the letter is now outdated and your significant other's feelings have changed since they wrote the letter and sent it in the mail?

I am guessing that most of you would not immediately jump to these questions. They honestly sound ridiculous and paranoid. If you trust your significant other, why would you have any reason to question their motives or authenticity? You also know your significant other and would be able to recognize their voice, their style, their tone, their nicknames for you, their inside jokes, and their references to moments you shared. It would be pretty easy to figure out if the letter was a fake because the letter just wouldn't sound like your significant other. Phrases would seem out of character; certain word choices would seem weird.

Well, the Bible is basically one giant love letter written for us by our heavenly Father. If we truly know God and trust His character, we should be able to read God's Word and decipher whether it is real or fake. Just like you are able to recognize your significant other's voice, we too should be able to recognize the voice of God. In reading through His Word, we should be able to see His character woven into the pages. Sections that might seem confusing to an outsider, should make more sense to us, because we have a history together with God that enables us to fill in the gaps, understand the context under which something was written, and connect scripture with our personal experiences with Him.

Now, if I had instead asked you to imagine getting a love letter in the mail from someone you just met or perhaps from someone you don't even know, it would totally make sense to be skeptical of that letter. Who in the world is this person? Why are they writing this? What are they talking about? What do they mean? The letter would be awkward, confusing, and downright creepy. No one in their right mind would read that letter and decide that they are now in love with the person who wrote the letter. It would be completely reasonable to question the letter's motives and authenticity, because you have no reason to trust the person who wrote that letter.

The question is then, How well do you know your heavenly Father? Do you recognize His voice? Can you tell when things are in alignment with His character? Can you decipher His voice over the many loud and blaring voices coming from society? In John 10:27 (ESV), Jesus says, "My sheep hear my voice, and I know them, and they follow me." Therefore, how in tune are you with your shepherd?

If you don't take the time to get to know God, how in the world are you going to understand God's Word and His character? Like any relationship, you get to know someone by spending time with them, doing things that they love, getting to know their friends and family, and engaging in conversation with them. Therefore, through prayer, serving others, and spending time in fellowship with other believers, you are able to get to know and understand God better. However, once you have done these things, how can you recognize the voice of God if you never even listen to His Word? It's like putting on noise-cancelling headphones and then complaining that you can't hear anything! You also must spend time reading God's Word so you can understand, for yourself, what God is truly saying.

The reality is there is a lot of confusion when it comes to the Bible, and to be blunt, most of it stems from ignorance. Most people do not take the time to get to know God, and even those who claim to know God, do not take the time to read His Word. As a result, most people are prone to view the Bible as some creepy letter from some random person they just met, rather than an intentional and sincere love letter from someone they love, admire, and respect. Their relationship with God is shallow and so when it is put to the test, they don't know what to believe, and their relationship starts to crumble.

According to *Christianity Today*, 18 percent of American churchgoers say that they *never* read the Bible.[4] What is astounding about this statistic is that it is talking about churchgoers, not Americans as a whole. These are individuals who are regularly attending church, supposedly hearing messages on the importance of scripture, and yet not taking the initiative to read the Bible on their own. Furthermore, according to LifeWay Research, 53 percent of Americans as a whole have read little to none of the Bible over the course of their life, meaning a little over half of Americans have virtually no knowledge of scripture, besides maybe a few Bible stories.[5]

---

[4] Russ Rankin, "Study: Bible Engagement in Churchgoers' Hearts, Not Always," *LifeWay Research*, January 1, 2014, https://www.lifeway.com/en/articles/research-survey-bible-engagement-churchgoers?carid=jhowe-stetzer-bible-20120913.

[5] Bob Smietana, "LifeWay Research: Americans Are Fond of the Bible, Don't Actually Read It," *LifeWay Research*, April 25, 2017, https://lifewayresearch.com/2017/04/25/lifeway-research-americans-are-fond-of-the-bible-dont-actually-read-it/

This statistic is shocking when you consider that almost 70 percent of Americans identify as Christians.[6] Additionally, these statistics are getting worse, as the number of US adults who never use the Bible on a regular basis has been steadily increasing over the past decade. Furthermore, when it comes to the millennial generation as a whole, 62 percent say that they have never read the Bible.[7]

Biblical illiteracy is therefore a stark reality that needs to be addressed. People like to make big claims about the Bible, its accuracy, and its relevance to modern-day society. However, the reality is most of those people don't have any idea what they are talking about. They are critical of a book they have never even read and are willing to take what others have to say about the Bible at face value without ever taking the initiative to study the Bible themselves.

Now, you may be asking yourself, What about those who do read the Bible regularly? Surely we can derive hope from the fact that 19 percent of American churchgoers do read the Bible daily, 39 percent read it on a weekly basis, and 22 percent on a monthly basis.[8] Additionally, around 20 percent of Americans as a whole have read the entire Bible at least once, and an additional 12 percent have read the Bible almost in its entirety.[9]

These statistics may seem a bit more encouraging; however, according to the Worldview Measurement Project conducted by the American Culture and Faith Institute, although 46 percent of Americans said that they had a biblical worldview, defined as individuals who "use the Bible as their filter for reality, to determine right from wrong, and to shape their beliefs, attitudes, and actions," in actuality, only 10 percent think and act according to biblical principles in their everyday lives.[10] What is worse is that when this statistic is broken down by generations, only 4 percent of

[6] "In U.S., Decline of Christianity Continues at Rapid Pace," *Pew Research Center*, October 17, 2019, https://www.pewforum.org/2019/10/17/in-u-s-decline-of-christianity-continues-at-rapid-pace/
[7] "Millennials and the Bible: 3 Surprising Insights," *Barna Research Group*, October 21, 2014, https://www.barna.com/research/millennials-and-the-bible-3-surprising-insights/
[8] Russ Rankin, "Study: Bible Engagement in Churchgoers' Hearts, Not Always."
[9] Bob Smietana, "LifeWay Research: Americans Are Fond of the Bible, Don't Actually Read It.".
[10] Avery Foley, "Study Shows Only 10% of Americans Have a Biblical Worldview," *Answers in Genesis*, May 2, 2017, https://answersingenesis.org/culture/study-shows-only-10-percent-americans-have-biblical-worldview/.

millennials say they have a biblical worldview and actually think and act through the lens of scripture.[11]

This discrepancy can be interpreted in a few different ways:

1) Americans who claim a biblical worldview are not actually reading scripture, so they don't actually know what it says (which is indeed evident to some extent from the other statistics presented above);

2) Americans who claim a biblical worldview and actively read scripture do not have an accurate understanding of what scripture says or means; or

3) Americans who claim a biblical worldview and actively read scripture understand what it says but choose not to believe or follow what the Bible says even though they still claim to follow a biblical worldview.

Either way, the result is what at least seems to be a multitude of hypocritical Christians who are claiming to have a biblical worldview without their actions reflecting that claim. No wonder Christians often get a bad rap; at least from an outsider's perspective, there seems to be little consensus and consistency on what it means to be a true biblical Christian and what it looks like to actively carry out a biblical worldview in the world today.

Therefore, of all these statistics, the one that I want you to really ponder is the fact that only around 10 percent of Americans (and only 4 percent of millennials) claim a biblical worldview and actually live it out. This small percentage of individuals are the ones who not only know and understand what scripture says but then choose to live by God's Word to the best of their ability. These individuals are not without sin and will make mistakes and fall short of what scripture says, but they are at least striving to be true to God's Word.

---

[11] Avery Foley. "Study Shows Only 10% of Americans Have a Biblical Worldview."

Let's then cut to the chase. Are you one of the 10 percent of Americans (or 4 percent of millennials) who claim a biblical worldview and actually live it out? Have you read God's Word for yourself (not just listened to what a pastor has said about it)? Do you understand what the Bible says? Do you take initiative to learn about the context and historical meaning of tricky passages? Do you actively try to apply scripture to your own life? Or, are you one of the 90 percent of Americans (or 96 percent of millennials) who don't know or understand the Bible or haven't taken steps to apply it to their lives? Do you criticize the Bible without really understanding it? Do you claim that the Bible is outdated and out of touch without knowing what it says and the historical context under which it was written?

Seriously, *no judgment* here, but I am guessing most of you are in the 90 percent (96 percent). Being a Christian is hard work. It is easy to become distracted by our day-to-day routines and the comforts and simple pleasures of this world. After a long day of work and the stresses of life, it is not our natural instinct to pick up God's Word and study it. In fact, we live in a culture that equates studying with doom, dread, and discouragement. Why would we voluntarily study something for fun?

Now, as a professor and former PhD student, I am probably part of the minority here who does actually think that studying is fun. I love to learn and am a sponge for knowledge. Listening to podcasts, reading articles and books, and learning new things are my hobbies. Therefore, I get it. Studying God's Word does not come naturally for most people; nor is it easy for any of us!

I want to make this clear though. My point here is not to say that everyone needs to go get a doctorate in theology and become hermits, studying God's Word. Thankfully, there are people out in the world who thrive off of knowledge and are willing to pour themselves over books, historical documents, archeological findings, dictionaries, and anthologies to churn out writings and teachings for others who do not have the access, time, skill sets, or natural inclinations to do so themselves. God created us all with different talents and giftings, and that is part of the beauty of His creation.

However, that being said, in Matthew 22:37, Jesus tells us to "love the Lord your God with all your heart and with all your soul and with all your mind." It is not enough to just have an emotional connection with Jesus, or even a spiritual one. We are also called to utilize our minds to further understand Jesus and His Word so we can love Him even more.

For example, for those of you who are huge fans of *The Bachelor* and *The Bachelorette* (like myself), think of how many times one of the leads ignores several major red flags and says something along the lines of "I just need to follow my heart." Meanwhile, Bachelor Nation is banging their head against the wall because it is so obvious that the lead is making the wrong choice. It is actually amazing how often the lead is blind to the fact that someone on the show is not there for the right reasons, or is the season's villain who can't seem to get along with anyone else in the house. It is obvious to everyone else, but the lead ignores all the facts in favor of an emotional connection. The few successful couples that come out of the Bachelor franchise are the ones who consider their emotional connection but also whether their lives and lifestyles are compatible, whether they share the same values, and so on. They use their heads in addition to their hearts.

When it comes to our relationship with Jesus, I am not trying to discount our emotional connection. Matthew 22 also tells us to love God with all our hearts as well as our souls and minds. Yet, as my favorite hymn ("Come Thou Fount") so aptly captures, our hearts are prone to wander. We are easily distracted, and we often lose sight of our goals. If we just have an emotional connection with God, the minute our lives turn upside down, or we have a bad day, it is easy to become disconnected from God.

However, if we work at using our hearts, souls, *and* minds to love Jesus, our foundation is not as easily shaken. The days when God feels distant and we are feeling down and discouraged, we can turn to our knowledge of God's Word and His character to renew our faith. Conversely, on days when we are struggling with tough questions about life and having a hard time reconciling God's Word with what we see going on in the world, we can lean into God's unfailing love for us to remind ourselves that we have a heavenly Father who is much bigger than our doubts, fears, and failures. Heart connection. Soul connection. Mind connection. All three working together in tandem to renew and reaffirm our relationship with God.

Therefore, we all need to be asking ourselves, What are the areas in our relationship with God that could use some more effort? It is easy to become lazy and complacent in our faith, but that makes us vulnerable to the lies of this world. When our faith is not grounded in biblical truth, we are far more likely to be pulled away from our faith. As a result, it is no surprise that in an era of biblical illiteracy, we are seeing people constantly fall away from the faith. There is a strong correlation between those who have actually read and studied their Bible and those who take their faith seriously, just like there is also a strong correlation between those who have barely cracked open their Bible and those who have walked away from God or are wishy-washy in their faith. Just like any relationship, you can't expect to never talk to or spend time with your significant other and expect the relationship to last.

WHAT OUR ITCHING EARS WANT TO HEAR...

It is one thing to actually start reading your Bible, but it is another thing entirely to actually believe scripture and do what it says. However, can we trust God's Word? Is God's Word outdated, or is it relevant to today's society? These are incredibly important questions, and I could get into the all the evidence and reasoning that demonstrates that the answer to these two questions is yes; however, there are much smarter and more knowledgeable people who have tackled these questions, and I would not be doing these questions justice by just dedicating a small, brief chapter to their answers. Instead, I encourage you to utilize your mind as discussed above and do research into these questions for yourself. I promise you that your world will be rocked and your love for Christ will increase the more you dig into how amazing God's Word is in its accuracy and relevancy.

Instead, I want to take a step back and look at the bigger picture here. The problem with our generation is not that we are incapable of understanding scripture or doing research on what scripture means and how it is relevant in today's society. We are incredibly tech savvy, are highly educated, and have access to more information than any other previous generation. In many ways, we should be far superior in our knowledge and understanding of scripture, given the access and resources available to us today. In fact, it is astounding that biblical illiteracy is so rampant, considering we have more access to biblical knowledge than ever before and have more evidence attesting to the Bible's accuracy and legitimacy than ever before as well.

The problem with Christians is that many of them don't want to study the Bible out of fear that they might have to then do what it says or change what they believe. Calling the Bible irrelevant and outdated is often a copout, an excuse made by people who don't want to sit down and study the Bible and possibly have to acknowledge that they might be wrong. It is far easier to cherry-pick a few nice-sounding verses to cling to, creating a hollow version of Christianity that is palatable for the masses, than actually dig into what the Bible says and find that the Bible asks a lot more out of us than just being a good person and praying every once in a while. The Bible is controversial and unpopular, and frankly, many people don't want to hear what it has to say.

In fact, according to research done by BARNA, when non-Christian millennials see someone reading the Bible in public, they assume that "the Bible reader is politically conservative (22%); that they don't have anything in common with the person (21%); that the Bible reader is old fashioned (17%); or that they are trying to make a statement or be provocative (15%)."[12] As someone who has frequently read my Bible in public, I can tell you that I am not trying to make a statement or be provocative, and I probably have a lot in common with most non-Christian millennials. However, the fact that something as innocent as reading your Bible in public elicits such a negative response is really telling to how people feel about the Bible and Christians today.

Furthermore, 19 percent of non-Christian millennials claim that the Bible is an outdated book with no relevance today, and 27 percent go as far to say that it is "a dangerous book of religious dogma used for centuries to oppress people."[13] In a 2018 article, *GQ* put together a list of "21 Books You Don't Have to Read," and number twelve was the Bible. In the article, the *GQ* editors wrote, "The Holy Bible is rated very highly by all the people who supposedly live by it but who in actuality have not read it. Those who have read it know there are some good parts, but overall, it is certainly not the finest thing that man has ever produced. It is repetitive, self-contradictory, sententious, foolish, and even at times ill-intentioned."[14]

---

[12] "Millennials and the Bible: 3 Surprising Insights." *Barna Research Group*

[13] "Millennials and the Bible: 3 Surprising Insights." *Barna Research Group.*

[14] "21 Books You Don't Have to Read." *GQ Magazine,* April 19, 2018. https://www.gq.com/story/21-books-you-dont-have-to-read

Not to dis on the editors of *GQ*, but last time I checked, their expertise was in men's fashion, style, grooming, fitness, and lifestyle rather than biblical theology. I highly doubt they cracked open a systematic theology book and used their hermeneutical principles before casting their judgment on the Bible. And yet they are not entirely off base in saying that people talk a big talk when it comes to the Bible, when they don't really know what they are talking about. Most people can quote John 3:16, but that doesn't mean they have read the Bible and understand what it actually says and means.

At the end of the day, however, ignorance is bliss. For Christians, it is simpler to know just the basics of scripture and not have to deal with any controversial or confusing passages. If you just stick to John 3:16, the golden rule, a few psalms and Proverbs, and the Christmas story of baby Jesus, you get a neatly packaged version of Christianity that makes you feel good and doesn't ruffle anyone's feathers. On the other hand, for non-Christians, it is easy to point to a few controversial passages of scripture on women, sexuality, slavery, or creation without understanding the historical context or how to interpret scripture and write off the whole Bible in its entirety. Taking the Bible seriously and actually studying it might cause you to change your opinions, or have to make some lifestyle changes, or think about big, important questions that make you feel uncomfortable. On both ends of the spectrum, it is easier to just stick with what you know and never critically engage the subject at all. Again, ignorance is bliss.

The Bible actually warns us about this. In 2 Timothy 4:2–4, it says, "Preach the word; be prepared in season and out of season; correct, rebuke and encourage—with great patience and careful instruction. For the time will come when people will not put up with sound doctrine. Instead, to suit their own desires, they will gather around them a great number of teachers to say what their itching ears want to hear."

The time has come when people are unwilling to put up with sound doctrine. Instead of seeking out truth, we gravitate toward people who tell us what our itching ears want to hear. We surround ourselves with like-minded individuals who believe the same things we do, creating echo chambers in which we are all just affirming what we already believe to be true about the world.

In fact, in 2016, *Oxford Dictionary* even declared "post-truth" to be the international word of the year after a 2,000 percent increase in its usage from the previous year. *Oxford Dictionary* defines post-truth as "relating to or denoting circumstances in which objective facts are less influential in shaping public opinion than appeals to emotion and personal belief." In a post-truth era, people cherry-pick the pieces of information that fit most closely with their beliefs about the world and are able to draw conclusions that are convenient and/or pleasing to them.

The term *post-truth* is most often associated with the trend of "fake news" that came out of the 2016 presidential election, but as a concept, it has been around for quite some time. People are now just starting to notice that living in a post-truth era is something we should be concerned about. There are consequences to society when people abandon an objective standard of truth.

Colossians 2:8 warns us about this as well. It says, "See to it that no one takes you captive through hollow and deceptive philosophy, which depends on human tradition and the elemental spiritual forces of this world rather than on Christ." In other words, you should be skeptical of things that sound good but are not fully rooted in truth. We all love a good inspirational quote, a poignant meme, a nice-sounding argument, a bumper sticker–worthy phrase. However, that means we also all need to be diligent in comparing how the wisdom of this world matches up with scripture. Just because an argument sounds nice doesn't mean it is scripturally accurate or in alignment with the character of Christ. Even scripture can be taken out of context to justify behavior or ideas that are not actually biblical. If we don't take the time to get to know God and His Word, we are only going to be increasingly susceptible to the half-truths of this world.

There is literally a spiritual battle going on against the dark powers of this world, and the one offensive weapon God gave us was His Word (Ephesians 6:10–17). Even when Jesus was being tempted in the desert by Satan, the only weapon He used to combat Satan was scripture (Matthew 4:1–11). Therefore, we do not serve a God who sends us out into battle with a flimsy, rubber sword. Matthew 4:4 says, "Man shall not live by bread alone, but on every word that comes from the mouth of God." God's Word is meant to sustain us, equip us, protect us, and rejuvenate us. It is all we really need. The problem is we are so quick to complain about its shortcomings before we even try it out or give it a chance.

I apologize in advance for using another Harry Potter analogy (although this is my last one, I promise), but it's like when Harry Potter is down in the Chamber of Secrets in the second book fighting for his life against Voldemort and a basilisk, and suddenly Dumbledore's phoenix arrives with the old sorting hat. Voldemort laughs and asks, "This is what Dumbledore sends his defender? A songbird and an old hat? … Let's match the power of Lord Voldemort, heir of Salazar Slytherin, against famous Harry Potter and the best weapons Dumbledore can give him."[15]

Even though Harry had no idea what Dumbledore had in mind, he knew that he was no longer alone. Lord Voldemort, however, was no longer laughing when the phoenix healed Harry's wounds with his tears, and Harry was able to pull the sword of Gryffindor out of the sorting hat to kill the basilisk. Contrary to what Voldemort thought, Dumbledore did not leave Harry hanging. Even though on the surface, the weapons Dumbledore gave Harry seemed useless, they were far more purposeful and powerful than anyone could have even imagined. They were exactly what Harry needed.

Therefore, why do we continue to underestimate the power of God and God's Word? Do we truly believe that the God of the universe is unable to properly equip us for being a follower of Christ? Do we honestly think that God would send us out to battle with flimsy rubber swords? We may not be privy to the entire battle plan, but we should be able to trust that when our commander sends us out into battle, He is going to give us the information and tools we need to be successful.

IT'S OK TO QUESTION GOD

Even as I write this, I can feel the resistance I am going to get from some of my readers. Mini alarm bells are probably going off in many of your heads. Young people today often have an issue with authority; we don't want to be told what to do, and we don't want to follow someone unconditionally. In some respects, this is a form of wisdom. We should not put our hope and trust in earthly forms of authority. However, we cannot put God in

---

[15] J. K. Rowling, *Harry Potter and the Chamber of Secrets* (New York: Scholastic, Inc., 2000)

the same category as earthly, sinful human authority figures. They are not the same! Somehow, we have to separate our baggage with authority figures from our relationship with Christ, the ultimate authority.

That being said, I am not calling us to have blind faith, to never ask questions, to become comfortable in our ignorance, or to never critically engage scripture. In fact, the Bible is pretty clear that our relationship with God and His Word should be active. Psalm 86:11 says, "Teach me your way, LORD, that I may rely on your faithfulness; give me an undivided heart, that I may fear your name." When things don't make sense, we should ask God to help us understand. When we have difficulty believing, we should ask God to increase our faith. When our hearts are divided, we should ask God to remind us of what is important. Psalm 119:18 then says, "Open my eyes, that I may see wonderful things in your law." In other words, make the Bible clear to me so I can see the meaning and benefit of scripture, even when I have doubts or frustration.

It is totally OK if we have questions or doubts. In fact, the Bible is full of people who questioned God. Job, a man described as "blameless and upright," whose life had been completely turned upside down, asks God many questions, including why Job was even born in the first place. Job literally lost everything and had every reason to be skeptical and cynical toward God. Nevertheless, Job still worshipped God along the way and trusted that God knew what He was doing even in the midst of his misery and confusion. Even though Job asked God many questions, seeking to understand, Job 1:22 says, "In all this, Job did not sin by charging God with wrongdoing." In other words, Job asked God why and implored God to make things clear to him, but in doing so, he did not call God's character into question.

Furthermore, when we read the psalms, we see that they are full of praises and worship of God, but they are also full of questions for God as well. "Why, LORD, do you stand far off? Why do you hide yourself in times of trouble?" (Psalm 10:1). "My soul is in deep anguish. How long, LORD, how long?" (Psalm 6:3). Then, in the New Testament, we see the disciples, who literally got to walk alongside Jesus and see Him at work, ask a million questions. However, Jesus continued to engage with them to help them understand His ways, even when the disciples doubted or were still confused.

Therefore, we can have doubts, ask questions, wonder why, and be confused when it comes to scripture and our relationship with the Lord. It is perfectly normal and expected and is even role-modelled to us throughout scripture. Our God is a personal God who finds joy in engaging with His children, teaching them along the way, and revealing parts of His plan to them when the time is right.

But the reality is this whole Christianity thing is an all-in or all-out deal. There is no in-between. In fact, God even expresses His disgust of lukewarm Christians. In Revelation 3:16 (ESV), God says, "So, because you are lukewarm, and neither hot nor cold, I will spit you out of my mouth." Being lukewarm gets us nowhere in the kingdom of heaven. We are being asked to pick a side, and I hope that you would think that being on the side of Christ is unbelievably worth it.

That being said, when we decide to be on God's side, we need to be all in. We either choose Jesus and all that comes with being a Christian, or we choose to be against Jesus. However, choosing to be with Jesus means choosing to be obedient to His Word. It is not like you are going to be able to stand before Jesus one day and say, "Hey, I read parts of that whole Bible thing, but I didn't like some parts, and other parts didn't make sense, so I just did things my way. I also think You made a couple of mistakes, and so I just went ahead and ignored them. Hope that is OK!"

It's like being the kid in school who tries to tell their teacher that the answer must be wrong because it's not the answer that they got. "Hey, teacher, I think your answer sheet must be wrong. Here you say that two plus two equals four, but when I added it up, I got five, so … can I at least get partial credit?" We can all think of at least one kid from school who was always trying to pull a fast one like that. Not only were they calling into question the authority of the teacher, but they were always trying to get credit for things they knew they did wrong.

God, however, doesn't give partial credit.

If we add up two plus two and get five, but the answer key says four, our response should be, "Wow, God, math is hard, and I clearly am not doing something right. Can you help me understand *why* two plus two equals four instead of five?" James 1:5–6 says, "If any of you lacks wisdom, you should ask God, who gives generously to all without finding fault, and it will be given to you. But when you ask, you must believe and not doubt, for the one who doubts is like a wave of the sea, blown and tossed by the wind." In other words, feel free to engage with God and ask Him anything, but do so from a place of humility, not from a place of pride. Furthermore, when you do ask God to make things clear to you, ask with a genuine desire to understand, rather than trying to justify your own behavior and beliefs.

For when we have a correct view of God, we have a correct understanding of our own limitations. Who are we to question the almighty God, the Creator of the universe? *And yet* the type of God we serve invites us to ask questions anyway because He desires to have a personal relationship with us. How surreal and amazing is that! Thus, the worst thing that we can do is to disengage, to turn our face from our heavenly Father, and to shut our ears to what He has to say. By dismissing the Word of God, we aren't even giving God a chance to help us understand what the Bible actually says. We are writing off scripture before we have even read it.

Therefore, I encourage you to read your Bible. Study what it says. Do your homework. Engage with other believers. Don't just blindly take at face value what people say about the Bible, when you haven't researched it for yourself. Ask God to clarify the parts of scripture that are difficult to understand. Talk to God about your doubts.

And then pray for a heart of obedience.

CHAPTER 4
WHY YOUNG ADULTS ARE LEAVING THE CHURCH—AND WHY THEY SHOULDN'T BE

When every creature finds its inmost melody
And every human heart its native cry
Oh then in one enraptured hymn of praise
We'll sing Christ be magnified

—"Christ be Magnified" by Cody Carnes

In 2018, church attendance in the United States dropped to an all-time low of 50 percent.[16] Whereas church membership in the US has traditionally hovered just over 70 percent, the past twenty years have witnessed a steep decline.[17] Some of this drop-off in church attendance can be attributed to the decline in the religiously affiliated population in the US, with now 19 percent of Americans claiming no religious affiliation, compared with only 8 percent approximately twenty years ago.[18] However, the increase in the number of religiously unaffiliated individuals in the US is not completely responsible for the drop-off in church attendance.

---

[16] Jeffrey M. Jones, "U.S. Church Membership Down Sharply in Past Two Decades," *Gallup*, April 18, 2019, https://news.gallup.com/poll/248837/church-membership-down-sharply-past-two-decades.aspx

[17] Jeffrey M. Jones, "U.S. Church Membership Down Sharply in Past Two Decades."

[18] Jeffrey M. Jones, "U.S. Church Membership Down Sharply in Past Two Decades."

Even among the religiously affiliated, church attendance is at an all-time low. In other words, being a Christian and going to church are not necessarily the same thing now in the US, whereas twenty-plus years ago, it was almost unthinkable to call yourself a Christian and then not go to church. In particular, church attendance is extremely low among millennials. Of millennials surveyed by Gallup between 2016 and 2018, only 42 percent of them went to church, in comparison to 68 percent of traditionalists, 57 percent of baby boomers, and 54 percent of Gen X'ers.[19] Even when just looking at millennials with a religious preference, only a little over a half of them are members of a church.[20]

So why are young adults leaving the church? In 2018, a popular article came out titled "59 Percent of Millennials Raised in a Church Have Dropped Out—And They're Trying to Tell Us Why." Now I first want to acknowledge that I believe this article to be well written and well intended, and it brings up some *very* important points that ring true. When I first read this article, my initial response was, *Can I get an amen?*

The article puts forth a long list of twelve reasons why millennials are leaving the church. It even provides action steps that the church can take to improve on these issues.[21]

1. *Nobody's Listening to Us*
2. *We're Sick of Hearing About Values & Mission Statements*
3. *Helping the Poor Isn't a Priority*
4. *We're Tired of You Blaming the Culture*
5. *The "You Can't Sit With Us" Affect*
6. *Distrust & Misallocation of Resources*
7. *We Want to Be Mentored, Not Preached At*
8. *We Want to Feel Valued*
9. *We Want You to Talk to Us About Controversial Issues (Because No One Is)*
10. *The Public Perception*

---

[19] Jeffrey M. Jones, "U.S. Church Membership Down Sharply in Past Two Decades."
[20] Jeffrey M. Jones, "U.S. Church Membership Down Sharply in Past Two Decades."
[21] Sam Eaton, "59 Percent of Millennials Raised in a Church Have Dropped Out—And They're Trying to Tell Us Why," *Faithit*, April 4, 2018, https://faithit.com/12-reasons-millennials-over-church-sam-eaton/

11. *Stop Talking About Us (Unless You're Actually Going to Do Something)*
12. *You're Failing to Adapt*[22]

Later in this chapter and later in this book, I am going to indirectly address many of the points raised above, because I think they are very important and worth discussing. However, before I do that, I want to first discuss how the author of this article ends her argument, because I think the tone of this article is very indicative of the highly dangerous attitude millennials have toward the church. The article concludes with the following statement:

> The truth is, church, it's your move. Decide if millennials actually matter to you and let us know if we should be leaving church. In the meantime, we'll be over here in our sweatpants listening to podcasts, serving the poor and agreeing with public opinion that perhaps church isn't as important or worthwhile as our parents have led us to believe.[23]

When I read this, I went from *Can I get an amen?* to *Wait—what?* Yes, there are a lot of ways the church can improve, and I agree that the church should be taking the initiative to adapt and address the needs and concerns of millennials. The church indeed needs to *be better.* However, sitting back and waiting for the church to make the first move is frankly lazy and self-indulgent. I know that we millennials hate the negative stereotypes targeted toward our generation, but this just feeds right into those stereotypes.

It is not surprising that, as millennials growing up with helicopter parents, we would blame the "adults" for not fixing our problems for us. Until mommy and daddy fix the church, I don't want to be a part of it. Our boycotting the church is like a pseudo temper tantrum. The church is not meeting our needs; therefore, we want nothing to do with it. However,

---

[22] Sam Eaton, "59 Percent of Millennials Raised in a Church Have Dropped Out—And They're Trying to Tell Us Why."

[23] Sam Eaton "59 Percent of Millennials Raised in a Church Have Dropped Out—And They're Trying to Tell Us Why."

instead of sitting back and complaining about the church, maybe we should be inside the church, instigating change from the inside out. Instead of asking what the church can do for you, ask what you can do for your church.

THE CHURCH IS THE BODY OF CHRIST

First of all, it is important to remember that the church is not a building, or a denomination, or an institution. The church is the body of Christ, of which Christ is the head. (Colossians 1:18, "And he is the head of the body, the church; he is the beginning and the firstborn from among the dead, so that in everything he might have the supremacy.") This means that regardless of your thoughts on church (as an institution), if you identify as a believer, you are part of the church, and the health of the church (a.k.a. the body of Christ) depends on all its parts working together.

It would be completely ridiculous if the legs said to the rest of the body, "Man, the rest of y'all need to get your stuff together. You are embarrassing us. While you figure your stuff out, I am going to remove myself from the body." Not to state the obvious, but 1) the body cannot be considered healed if it is missing its legs. 2) The legs can't go off on their own and magically make their own new body. 3) If the legs truly separated themselves from the body, the body would start hemorrhaging and die. How's that for a visual?

The point is if as young adults we decide to remove ourselves from the body of Christ, we are not only hurting the body, but we are also separating ourselves from Christ, who is the head of the body. Instead, what if the arms, legs, neck, spine, stomach, ribcage, fingernails, toes, and funny bones all looked to the head of the body for guidance and direction on how the body should look and act? What if we were all singing the same song of praise with the purpose of magnifying Christ and His perfect glory, instead of pointing the finger at one another and tearing the body of Christ apart?

Church (as an institution) and the church (as a community of believers) are indeed both flawed and in desperate need of healing. We unfortunately are still facing the consequences of the Fall. For thousands of years, God's original plan for creation has continued to be distorted and destroyed by imperfect human beings, and the reality is it will continue to be distorted and destroyed until Jesus returns. In the meantime, Christ gave us tools for survival to help us not become discouraged or cynical: biblical community (a.k.a. the church) and the Holy Spirit.

As Hebrews 10:24–25 states, "Let us consider how we may spur one another on toward love and good deeds, *not giving up meeting together*, as some are in the habit of doing, but encouraging one another—and all the more as you see the Day approaching." The Bible tells us that we are going to face difficult times both now and in the future. The good news is that we were not meant as believers to face these challenges alone, even though it may be tempting to isolate ourselves when we are frustrated, fearful, or fatigued. As the verses in Hebrews above suggest, even early Christians were also tempted to stop meeting together and going to church. However, they were actually facing real persecution that could cost them their lives. Today, we may face persecution in the sense that we are unfairly judged or made fun of, but we experience only a fraction of the level of persecution believers in the early church faced or even Christians around the world today. We are so afraid of being associated with the church today, out of fear for being stereotyped as judgmental, close-minded, or out of touch. Although, imagine the fear early Christians faced for their association with the church. Our fear is so shallow in comparison.

The reality is it is easier to become cynical and critical when we aren't being spurred on by our fellow believers. It is not a surprise that those who are the most cynical and critical are the ones who are not actually in the church and are not surrounded by fellow believers. It is easy to criticize from a distance, especially in an age where we can hide behind the comfort of social media. However, our isolation and cynicism are not helpful for our own personal edification or for bringing glory to Christ. As believers, we are supposed to be light in this world. Matthew 5:14–16 says, "You are the light of the world. A town built on a hill cannot be hidden. Neither do people light a lamp and put it under a bowl. Instead they put it on its stand, and it gives light to everyone in the house. In the same way, let your light shine before others, that they may see your good deeds and glorify your Father in heaven." When the world looks at believers, they should see a symbol of hope and a reflection of our heavenly Father, not a picture of bitterness and darkness.

Let me take this analogy further though. Although we are all called to be the light of the world, unfortunately not all lights shine with the same brightness. Imagine a light bulb that is getting dim. If that light bulb is in a completely dark room, that light bulb, relatively speaking, is still the brightest thing in the room. However, if that light bulb was placed in a room of other light bulbs, it might be one of the least bright things in the room. Similarly, when we are surrounded in darkness, often because of our own isolation and cynicism, we may not notice that our light is getting dim because, relatively speaking, we have nothing to compare it to. As a result, we often allow ourselves to become lulled into a false sense of security, wanting to believe that we are still representing Christ in the darkness, not realizing how far we have strayed. Additionally, what no one wants to admit is that we may even like staying in darkness because we like the feeling of being the brightest thing in the room, rather than the dimmest. We don't want to return to the light out of fear of being exposed for how dim our lights have become.

As believers though, we are called to both be in community and to go out into the world to be a witness for Christ. Therefore, we need to come together with other believers for a regular tune-up, especially when our lights are getting dim. Only then can we be fully equipped to go out as a light into the darkness. If, though, we remain in the darkness and our light starts to go out, we may not even notice, and we might not be able to find our way back to the light.

Our isolation from other believers is one of the worst things we can do in our walk with Christ. We were not designed to do this whole Christianity thing on our own. As Proverbs 27:17 states, "As iron sharpens iron, so one person sharpens another." We cannot progress in our faith without the support of other believers. Christian fellowship is crucial for accountability, encouragement, discipleship, and worship, and it is the church's job to facilitate opportunities for these relationships to flourish. For those who have left the church, they have pretty much cut themselves off from Christian fellowship. Sure, they may have conversations about faith with a friend here and there, but most of the time, there is a complete lack of intentional time spent with other believers for the purpose of growing deeper in their faith. As a result, it is not surprising that their faith becomes stagnant. In fact, I have never met a believer who is on fire for God and experiencing spiritual growth who was not also regularly and intentionally engaged with other believers.

Now I get it. There have been times in my life when I have dragged my feet going to church, or I have been reluctant to add one more thing to my very busy schedule. There have been times when I have been very critical of Christian community and have found it easier to disengage rather than show up and put in the hard work of transforming myself as well as the body of Christ. I have gone to church events that have been just downright painful, and I have definitely had my fair share of cringe-worthy church experiences. Christians can be incredibly awkward; community events can sometimes feel forced; sometimes the pastor says something totally out of left field; worship can feel outdated and disingenuous.

The fact of the matter is many people have not had good church experiences, which is why many of them are reluctant to return. The church they attended was maybe too old-fashioned or not young or hip enough. It was maybe too touchy-feely or maybe even too cold and impersonal. Maybe no one even talked to them, and they left feeling isolated and ignored, or maybe too many people talked to them, and they couldn't get out of there fast enough. They maybe felt that everyone was too superficial and fake, speaking in platitudes without any substance, or maybe they felt that people were too vulnerable and were oversharing. And maybe they even felt judged or unwelcome, or worse, mistreated or abused.

Therefore, it is tempting to say that church is not necessary, especially if we have had painful or awkward church experiences that we didn't get much out of. Although it is true that your salvation is not dependent on you going to church every Sunday, it is also true that God created us to be in community with other believers. You are far more likely to walk away from the faith if you are surrounded by nonbelievers than if you are surrounded by your brothers and sisters in Christ. As 1 Corinthians 15:33 puts it, "Bad company corrupts good character." Who is there to encourage you? Who is there to hold you accountable? Who is there to pray for you?

This is exactly why we need the church. Our faith cannot survive on its own. We need both other believers *and* the Holy Spirit to revitalize our faith. In Matthew 18:20, Jesus tells us that "where two or three gather in my name, there am I with them." He is not saying that He is absent in our lives until we gather together with others but is reminding us that community is important, and Jesus values and works through relationships. He knows that oftentimes more work can be done for the kingdom when we work together. The Holy Spirit can be accessed on a whole different level when we come together as believers.

THE CHURCH NEEDS YOUNG PEOPLE

So, are there issues with the church? Absolutely. Does the American church need to undergo a massive transformation? You betcha! However, change is not going to come from boycotting the church. Young adult ministries across the country are going extinct, not because they aren't important but because young people are just not showing up. And the fact of the matter is even though many young adults might say that they are boycotting the church out of principle, in reality, most young people are not in the church because they are too busy focusing on their careers, are not willing to give up social activities with friends, are distracted by social media and TV shows and idolizing self-care time, or are simply distant from God and dry in their faith. Christian community is no longer a priority in their lives.

This perpetuates a vicious cycle. If young adults never show up, churches are going to stop catering to the needs of young adults and wasting precious resources on a population that is flaky and disinterested. But then, on the rare occasion that young adults actually do show up, these young adults complain because the church is outdated and not meeting their needs. They then leave the church before any changes can be made. As a result, the church continues to cater to its primary population that is mostly families or older people. In doing so, a large population of young people, who are in some of the most formative years of their lives, are virtually receiving no Christian teaching, fellowship, or mentorship. Is it the church's fault? Yes. Is it also the fault of a generation of "believers" who have removed themselves from the church? Also, yes.

What if young people truly valued the importance of Christian community and committed themselves to seeking out fellowship, mentorship, and even leadership opportunities? You could even start small. Maybe the first thing you need to do is find a friend or two in your life who also are believers and ask them to start going to church with you. You can then even start your own small group to discuss the Bible or the message you heard on Sunday. Or maybe you could join a ministry team to serve your community alongside fellow believers.

The more involved you are in your local church and the more connected you become to the Christian community, the more opportunities you have to speak up, initiate change, and call out areas where the church is falling short. You gotta start somewhere though. It does nobody any good to just sit on the sidelines.

For example, when my husband and I first moved to the Bay Area, we had very little Christian community. Other than a handful of college friends who were spread out around the Bay, we virtually knew no one and were starting from scratch. It was important to us to be a part of a church community, so we started going to a church in our area. We knew that we were never going to get to know people or get connected if we just showed up on Sundays, and so literally the second Sunday we were there, we marched right up to the high school ministry room and asked how we could get involved.

Like most church ministries, they were in desperate need of volunteers, and so after a quick interview to make sure we were serious believers who could be trusted, they asked us to join the team. Two weeks later, we were already headed off to Hume Lake's Winter Camp with almost two hundred high schoolers to serve as camp counselors. We didn't tiptoe around the idea of getting involved; we just dove right in.

As a result, joining high school ministry was one of the best decisions my husband and I could have made. The other high school leaders became some of our best friends, and serving and doing life alongside other believers was incredibly life giving for our faiths. We also became really close with an older married couple in the church whose kids were in our high school group, and they became mentor figures for us. It was the first time since college that we really felt poured into by believers who were further along in their faiths. In addition to high school ministry, we also got plugged in with a men's and women's Bible study that also provided awesome opportunities for mentorship, accountability, and growth.

My husband and I found that the more we got involved in our church, the more connected we became. Even though our church was home to several thousand people, it actually felt really small. Through our involvement in the church, we also started to get to know the church leadership team. As a result, we were invited to vision-casting sessions for the church and even got a chance to sit down with one of the senior pastors who wanted to hear our opinions on how the church could improve in meeting the needs of young people. We felt valued for our perspective and contribution to the larger church community and were never belittled because of our age but rather were celebrated for it.

The church needs young people and the perspectives they can bring. First Timothy 4:12 says, "Don't let anyone look down on you because you are young, but set an example for the believers in speech, in conduct, in love, in faith and in purity." We are, therefore, called by scripture as young people to set an example, to offer a fresh perspective, especially when older generations have become hardened in their faiths.

We are so quick to point the finger at other generations, blaming them for everything that is wrong with the church and world. However, we are not the first generation that has thought that our parents' generation was outdated and out of touch. Furthermore, our parents' generation isn't the first generation that has thought that these wild youngins are messing up all their hard work.

The reality is God created everything with a purpose. There is a reason why we will all eventually get old and a new generation will eventually come in to take our place. Ecclesiastes 3 tells us that there is a time for everything, a time to plant, and a time to uproot. However, who is going to do the work of planting and uprooting? It is difficult, hands-on work that cannot be done at a distance. It also takes time and patience, which can be difficult for young people who want change to happen now. Although, our energy and fresh perspective are just what the church needs to make these necessary changes.

As I mentioned at the start of this chapter, I plan to discuss many of the issues that are wrong with the American church later in this book. So don't worry—I am not letting the church off the hook! However, these issues cannot be addressed if we do not understand why the church is important in the first place. Why fix something that has little to no value in our lives? Why complain about something that we could care less about?

We are so quick to treat the church like some brand that is going out of style, but the church is not a product that is for sale, and nor should it be! When the purpose of the church becomes too focused on how it can attract new members and make them stay, the church is missing the point. It is not as if the church is a sorority or fraternity that must decide how it is going to attract new recruits each year in order to stay competitive with the other sororities and fraternities. We do not want the church to be susceptible to worldly trends and fads. Your participation in the church should not be dependent on how well the church has won your business.

The church is instead a family made up of brothers and sisters in Christ. Like it or not, you are either part of the family, or you are not. Sure, you might be embarrassed by your family at times and may even have to call them out to initiate change. But the health of the family is contingent upon all members being willing to participate. Everyone has a role to play, and it is important to recognize what your role may be. However, I can tell you right now that standing from the sidelines, pointing the finger at the church from the outside is *not* your spiritual calling. Removing yourself from the church is equivalent to saying that you no longer want to be part of God's family. It is a personal attack against God.

The good news about God's family is that it is literally open to everyone, meaning that we *all* have a chance to be adopted into the kingdom of heaven and receive the free gift of salvation. The bad news is people secretly deep down don't want God's family to be open to everyone. They only want it to be open to the people they like who aren't rough around the edges, don't say foolish things, follow the rules, aren't ignorant or arrogant, aren't weird or politically incorrect, have it all together, and don't make everyone else look bad. People do not want to believe that God loves their weird racist uncle or totally out there, free-spirited hippie aunt as much as He loves them.

But that is not how God works. The beauty of God's family is that it is judged based on Christ's perfect sacrifice, not our own shortcomings. Our areas of weakness are opportunities for God's glory to shine through. Second Corinthians 12:9 tells us that Christ's power is made perfect in weakness. Despite the fact that the church is messed up and consistently falls short, God still chooses to meet us where we are at. Our unity as the body of Christ magnifies God's greatness, not our own. Hate to burst your bubble, but God can use your weird racist uncle or totally out there, free-spirited hippie aunt just as much as He can use you. Therefore, who are we to diminish the power of Christ through our own personal condemnation of His family?

This is not to excuse the sins of the church or justify the behavior of its members. I truly believe that there are some serious issues with the church that need to be fixed. However, we do need to ask ourselves whether we are more concerned about our own reputation as believers or about Christ's reputation? By removing ourselves from the church, we are essentially saying that being a part of God's family isn't all that it is cracked up to be. We are so willing to sacrifice Christ's reputation for the sake of our own. As believers, we have lost our sense of family loyalty, purposefully stirring up disunity in the body of Christ.

What then is more loving? To cut ourselves off from someone, claiming that they are a lost cause, or to continue the tedious, hard work of showing up daily to help someone make the necessary changes in their life that are for their own good? Is the church (a.k.a. the body of Christ) a lost cause? Or is it worth showing up daily to help the church make the necessary changes? As believers, we were not called to sit on the sidelines or criticize at a distance. Instead, we should be on the front lines, doing real kingdom work, rather than defecting from the cause itself.

However, we are living in an age where we have come to accept a dismembered body of Christ. We have excused parts of the body for going off and doing their own thing, forgetting that the body can only effectively operate when all members of the body are working together through the guidance and direction of Christ, who is the head. In doing so, those who have effectively left the church (and the body of Christ) have developed a false sense of moral superiority, patting themselves on the back for deserting the rest of the body. They sit back and criticize the body for hemorrhaging, forgetting that their self-removal from the body is also responsible for tearing the body apart.

Therefore, we can sit back and criticize the sinking ship that is the church, forgetting that we are ~~also~~ drowning as well, or we can humble ourselves and recognize that all our issues with the church are not going to be solved until all members of the body recognize that the church is worth saving. Then, as members of the connected body look to Christ for their leadership, church healing and transformation can begin.

CHAPTER 5
JUDGY, JUDGY CHRISTIANS

Come out of hiding
You're safe here with Me
There's no need to cover
What I already see
You've got your reasons
But I hold your peace
You've been on lock-down
And I hold the key
'Cause I loved you before you knew it was love
And I saw it all, still I chose the cross

—"Out of Hiding (Father's Song)" by Steffany Gretzinger

In today's world, being described as judgmental is one of the worst insults a person can receive. Tolerance is idolized as the ideal, and proselytizing your belief system is now extremely taboo in society. By the world's standards, telling someone that their beliefs or way of life is wrong is considered to be borderline blasphemy.

Unfortunately for Christians, we have developed a reputation for being judgmental, which has made us extremely unpopular in modern-day society. According to a recent study done by BARNA, "substantial majorities of Millennials who don't go to church say they see Christians as judgmental (87%), hypocritical (85%), anti-homosexual (91%) and insensitive to others

(70%)."[24] As a result, I honestly feel like I am constantly engaged in some form of damage control around nonbelievers, hoping I can change their opinion of Christians. It can be extremely frustrating because it often feels like the minute you make any progress with a nonbeliever, there is another news story that comes out about a Christian doing something incredibly insensitive, judgmental, or ignorant, and you are back at square one.

The reality is for every negative news story that comes out about Christians, there are probably hundreds more positive stories, but those aren't the stories we hear because those stories don't sell. That means, as Christians, we often have to work even harder to overcome people's negative opinions of us so that we are still able to demonstrate the love of Christ. I wish I had some statistics on this, but I bet you that most people actually have really positive interactions with the Christians they know personally in their lives, but one bad interaction or memorable news story can make someone forget all the good interactions they have had. What is probably even more likely is that most people don't even know who the Christians are in their lives because Christians are afraid to speak up out of fear of being labeled as "that judgmental Christian guy (or girl)." As a result, people might not even know that they are having positive interactions with Christians on a daily basis.

The fact of the matter is, however, that there is an inherent contradiction in today's society. We are encouraged to speak our truth and to be tolerant of other people's beliefs and actions. In contrast, people who advocate for one truth are seen as narrow-minded and judgmental. However, *truth* according to *Oxford Dictionary* is defined as "that which is true or in accordance with fact or reality." Even though we are trying to make truth a relative concept, by definition, truth has an objectivity that cannot be ignored. Something is either true or false. It is either based in fact, or it is not.

Therefore, what happens when my truth contradicts your truth? Can they both still be true? Is one truth more valid than the other? These are the types of questions that are embedded in today's society, but they

---

[24] "What Millennials Want When They Visit Church," *Barna Group*, March 4, 2015, https://www.barna.com/research/what-millennials-want-when-they-visit-church/

distract us from the most important questions, such as, What is truth? What is true, and what is false? What is right, and what is wrong?

In 2005, an article came out in the *East Bay Times* about a couple who took their two-year-old twin daughters to an S&M festival in San Francisco. Surrounded by naked people and people in fetish costumes, showcasing bondage, whipping, flogging, and spanking, these two toddlers were unfortunately not the only children at the event. Upon being asked whether it was appropriate to bring their young children to the festival, the parents of the twin girls stated, "Every parent has to decide for themselves what is right for them. And I respect that. And we decided that this is right for our children."[25]

This is obviously (and intentionally) an extreme example, but it raises some very important questions. In a world of "you do you" and "speak your own truth," are we allowed to tell these parents that their choice to expose their young daughters to the S&M culture is wrong? I think (and hope) that most people would agree that this is a form of sexual abuse and that these parents should not be allowed to expose their children to pornography without consequences. This is because most people have a general sense of right and wrong, and this situation screams all kinds of wrong.

However, as evidenced by the comments of this particular couple, not all people believe there is an objective standard of right and wrong. Instead, they believe that right and wrong are relative concepts that have different definitions depending on who you ask. Some people think that bringing kids to an S&M festival is wrong, and others think it is okay, just like some people prefer chocolate, and others vanilla. What is "right" for their children may be different from what is "right" for our children, and we should respect these differences. In this view, telling this couple that it is wrong to take their daughters to the S&M festival is considered close-minded and judgmental.

Now if I told you the same story, but the festival was a vegetarian convention or a homeschooling celebration, you might have a different

---

[25] William Love and Poh Si Teng, "Folsom: a perfect place for kids?" *East Bay Times,* September 25, 2005, https://www.eastbaytimes.com/2005/09/29/folsom-a-perfect-place-for-kids/

reaction. I might be a meat-loving mom who is a huge advocate of the public school system, but who am I to judge? You do you …

Do you see the problem here? Where do we draw the line between when it is OK to judge and when you should keep your mouth shut? There are some things that almost everyone agrees are wrong (e.g., murder, sexual abuse, child pornography, etc.), and these things tend to already be covered by the law. Therefore, there is often a moral justification and a legal justification to judge these actions. On the other end of the spectrum, there are lifestyle differences that aren't harming anyone, that most people are OK with accepting, even though they personally might have different preferences.

However, what about the stuff in the middle? Religion? Politics? The stuff we aren't "supposed" to talk about, even though most people still do. Where is the cutoff point? When do we crossover from lifestyle choices to questions of morality? When should we sit back and let people "speak their truth" and do what they think is right for them and their family, and when are we called to step in and say something, to stand up for what we think is right? When is tolerance a noble cause, and when is being tolerant a euphemism for apathy or complicity?

I find it to be incredibly ironic that as much as Americans today like to proclaim the gospel of tolerance, when the chips are down, most people aren't very tolerant of others, particularly when it comes to different belief systems. The reality is we want people to be tolerant of our lifestyle choices and beliefs, but at the same time, we often want everyone to think and act the same way we do. In other words, we advocate for tolerance when it comes to people whom we agree with, but when we disagree, we want to step in under the guise of doing the right thing and speaking our truth. Thus, if we are really honest with ourselves, the doctrine of tolerance is not without conditions.

For example, it comes as no surprise that in regard to people's political beliefs, political polarization is at an all-time high and has amplified feelings of animosity between people from different political parties. Today, 58 percent of Republicans and 55 percent of Democrats have a *very* unfavorable opinion about members of the opposite party.[26] Since the 1950s, the number of Democrats and Republicans who want their child to marry someone from the same political party has dramatically increased (an increase from 33 percent to 60 percent of Democrats between 1958 and 2016 and an increase from 25 percent to 63 percent of Republicans between 1958 and 2016).[27] Forty-five percent of Republicans and 41 percent of Democrats view the policies of the other party as a threat to society.[28]

A recent study also found that after the 2016 election, just over 42 percent of Republicans and Democrats believed that members of the opposite political party were not just bad for politics but were downright evil.[29] In addition, one out of five Democrats and Republicans believed that members of the opposite political party "lack the traits to be considered fully human—they behave like animals."[30] Even more appalling, 20 percent of Democrats and 16 percent of Republicans surveyed believed that the country would be better off if a large portion of the opposing political party just died off.[31]

Now it is important to note that individuals who take surveys are sometimes more likely to express more extreme views, so these statistics are likely a bit inflated, but the fact of the matter is there is a growing population in the United States (on both sides of the political spectrum) who are extremely judgmental and intolerant of the political beliefs of others. Our political beliefs have become synonymous with our standards of morality. Thus, if you vote differently than me, you must be less moral. As a result, it is then my duty to step in and correct you in order to turn you from your ignorant and/or evil ways.

---

[26] Carroll Doherty and Jocelyn Kiley, "Key facts about partisanship and political animosity in America," *PEW Research Center,* June 22, 2016, https://www.pewresearch.org/fact-tank/2016/06/22/key-facts-partisanship/

[27] Lynn Vavreck, "A Measure of Identity: Are You Wedded to Your Party?" *New York Times,* January 31, 2017, https://www.nytimes.com/2017/01/31/upshot/are-you-married-to-your-party.html

[28] Carroll Doherty and Jocelyn Kiley, "Key facts about partisanship and political animosity in America."

[29] Thomas B. Edsall, "No Hate Left Behind," *New York Times,* March 13, 2019, https://www.nytimes.com/2019/03/13/opinion/hate-politics.html

[30] Thomas B. Edsall, "No Hate Left Behind."

[31] Thomas B. Edsall, "No Hate Left Behind."

The same is true when it comes to people's religious beliefs. I also find it ironic that many people who hold tolerance in such high esteem are not very tolerant of the beliefs and practices of Christians in particular. The same people who idolize the doctrine of tolerance are often extremely intolerant of the Christian worldview, criticizing it for being too close-minded and judgmental. As a result, Christians are often the only ones who are not praised for "speaking their truth."

In fact, a recent study of Americans demonstrated that 75 percent of Americans believe that "being religiously extreme is a threat to society."[32] Now, you might think that being religiously extreme includes things like religious terrorism, religious fanaticism, religious isolation, and so on, and I am sure that a good portion of that 75 percent had those types of things in mind when they said that "being religiously extreme is a threat to society." However, that same study demonstrated that many of Americans view the regular religious practices of traditional religious groups to be "extreme."[33]

For example, 60 percent of Americans view evangelism to be "extreme."[34] Fifty-one percent believe that individuals who "protest government policies that conflict with their 'religion' are 'extreme.'"[35] Additionally, 42 percent believe that quitting your job to do missions work in another country is "extreme," and 25 percent believe that abstaining from sex until marriage is "extreme."[36] What is interesting about this rhetoric is that the use of the word *extreme* somehow implies that individuals "who advocate for sexual abstinence or value missions work over money constitute, in some way, a social threat."[37] What was normally considered to be regular and harmless religious practices are increasingly being viewed as not only countercultural but as dangerous.

Therefore, on the one hand, we want to honor individual liberty and respect the religious beliefs of others. On the other hand, we are highly suspicious of individuals who express different beliefs than ourselves and

---

[32] Jonathan Merritt, "Are Conservative Christians 'Religious Extremists'?" *The Atlantic,* March 10, 2016, https://www.theatlantic.com/politics/archive/2016/03/are-conservative-christians-religious-extremists/473187/

[33] Jonathan Merritt, "Are Conservative Christians 'Religious Extremists'?"

[34] Jonathan Merritt, "Are Conservative Christians 'Religious Extremists'?"

[35] Jonathan Merritt, "Are Conservative Christians 'Religious Extremists'?"

[36] Jonathan Merritt, "Are Conservative Christians 'Religious Extremists'?"

[37] Jonathan, Merritt, "Are Conservative Christians 'Religious Extremists'?"

are worried that if people actually take their beliefs seriously, they might infringe upon the beliefs of ourselves or others. As a result, we are tolerant but only to a certain point.

Still confused then on the issue of tolerance and when you should step in and say something and when you should keep your mouth shut? Don't worry. Me too. Tolerance really only works with lukewarm belief systems that won't actually result in any action. It's like telling people they can bring any type of salsa that they want to the party, as long as it is mild and from a particular brand.

Thus, the doctrine of tolerance sounds nice and often has noble intentions, but the fact of the matter is tolerance is oftentimes incompatible with righteousness. Proverbs 14:12 says, "There is a way that seems right to a man, but its end is the way to death." We were not called to stay silent. We were not called to turn a blind eye. We were not called to sit back and watch God's children march off on the path to destruction. Jesus did not come to this earth so that people could just go on living their lives as they see fit without any consequences.

Therefore, the issue is not whether we should speak up but when and how we should speak up as Christians. Ecclesiastes 3:7 even tells us that there is a time to stay silent and a time to speak. Thus, there is wisdom in knowing that our words are not always helpful and that sometimes we can do more damage by speaking up. Proverbs 21:23 says, "Those who guard their mouths and their tongues keep themselves from calamity." In addition, there is also wisdom in knowing that there are some who are not ready to hear what we have to say. Proverbs 23:9 (NLT) tells us, "Don't waste your breath on fools, for they will despise the wisest advice." In other words, we need to learn how to pick our battles and not waste our time and energy on arguing with people whose hearts have been hardened.

I wish I could say that I have perfected this wisdom myself, but the reality is developing this type of wisdom is a process that requires a *ton* of prayer and the Holy Spirit's prompting. Before saying anything to anyone (or posting anything on social media), you should first ask God if you should speak or stay silent. Ask God for the right words to say if He does ask you to speak up. Ask God to prepare the hearts of those whom you are planning on speaking with. Ask God for a spirit of gentleness and humility. Ask God to give you compassion.

Whether you are engaging in a conversation with a believer or a nonbeliever, you want the conversation to be spirit led. You want the words coming out of your mouth to be from God, not from your own prideful thoughts. You want to speak in a spirit of gentleness and kindness that, above all else, honors Christ in both your words and actions. You want to speak not out of impulse but out of intentionality. Philippians 4:5 (ESV) tells us, "Let your reasonableness be known to everyone," and Titus 3:2 (ESV) tells us to be ready to "show perfect courtesy toward all people." If you are not prepared to do those things, it is best if you remain silent.

However, knowing when to hold our tongue does not mean that we should never speak up. Many of you have probably heard the verse in Matthew that says, "Judge not, that you be not judged." It is easy to remember and sounds nice when you say it. It is a great verse to combat your nonbeliever friends who claim that Christians are too judgmental. It is easy to point to it and say, "See? Even the Bible says we shouldn't be judgmental!" However, most people have not read the entire passage that this verse comes from.

Matthew 7:1–6 (ESV) says this in its entirety:

> Judge not, that you be not judged. For with the judgment you pronounce you will be judged, and with the measure you use it will be measured to you. Why do you see the speck that is in your brother's eye, but do not notice the log that is in your own eye? Or how can you say to your brother, "Let me take the speck out of your eye," when there is the log in your own eye? *You hypocrite, first take the log out of your own eye, and then you will see clearly to take the speck out of your brother's eye.* (emphasis added)

The Bible is pretty clear that it is not our job to point the finger and condemn people. In fact, the passage above is fairly clear that being judgmental will result in even greater judgment for ourselves when we get to heaven. Yikes! Our first concern should be dealing with our own sin, which requires us to humble ourselves and recognize our own shortcomings. However, the passage does not stop there. It continues on to say that once

Not the point.

you have taken the log out of your own eye, "you will see clearly to take the speck out of your brother's eye."

Here scripture is not saying that we should just live our lives, turning a blind eye to one another's sin. This passage is a beautiful picture of humility, then companionship. It is first and foremost a call to examine your own life and your own areas of sin. If you don't take the log out of your own eye, you are not in a position to help your fellow brother. Once you do take the log out of your own eye, however, you are not only more credible, but also you have the compassion and vantage point to help a fellow brother or sister.

For example, there is a reason why Alcoholics Anonymous (AA) uses individuals who have completed their twelve-step program successfully as sponsors for new members. Having someone who can say that they have been there, that they have walked through what you are going through, is incredibly powerful. The sponsors get it. They aren't just some sober person who is trying to tell an alcoholic to get better. If someone were to say to an alcoholic, "Just stop drinking. Don't you want to be sober? It's not that hard. Mind over matter here," they would come across not only as incredibly insensitive but also ignorant and naive. Instead, having someone who is able to say, "No judgment here at all. I have been there. I was in your shoes not too long ago, and it was an incredibly difficult season of my life. Let me come alongside you and support you in this journey as someone who truly understands what you are going through," is both meaningful and powerful.

Galatians 6:1–2 (ESV) says: "Brothers, if anyone is caught in any transgression, you who are spiritual should restore him in a spirit of gentleness. Keep watch on yourself, lest you too be tempted. Bear one another's burdens, and so fulfill the law of Christ." This verse tells us that if we are to call one another out in sin, we are called to do it in a spirit of gentleness, not one of critique and judgment. Furthermore, we are then called to bear one another's burdens. Imagine what the world would look like if instead of pointing the finger, Christians came alongside people in their sin with empathy and compassion and said, "Here, let me walk through this with you. You do not have to go through this alone. I too have stumbled and have needed a friend to help me back up. Let me be that friend to you."

In addition, this verse in Galatians also reminds us that, at any point, we are vulnerable to temptation as well. Even as we walk alongside our fellow believers, we can also stumble; therefore, we must all be vigilant as we partner with one another to flee temptation and strive for righteousness in our lives. You may help a brother or sister today, knowing that they might need to help you tomorrow. Holiness is a daily decision; it is not something that we either have or have not already achieved. Every day, we fall short, and when we are keen to remember that, we are able to empathize with the shortcomings of our fellow believers.

The problem is, when it comes to sin, people like to create a hierarchy in which some sins are "worse" than others. In other words, most people like to think that they are the one with the speck in their eye, while everyone else has a log in theirs. They then find comfort in the fact that they at least don't have a log in their eye and feel a moral obligation to help all those poor people with logs in their eyes.

However, that is not how the passage in Matthew was written. When you recognize the full weight of your sin, you should feel like there is a log in your eye. It should be a humbling experience. When you have a log in your eye, you can't even see the speck in your brother's eye. Deal with your own sin first, and then from a place of humility and compassion, you can walk alongside a brother or sister who is struggling.

A CRITICAL DISTINCTION: BELIEVERS WITHIN THE CHURCH VERSUS NONBELIEVERS OUTSIDE THE CHURCH

It is important to distinguish here though that there is a *major* difference between calling out your fellow believers in their sin and condemning people outside the church in their sin. Here is where I think a lot of Christians get confused. It is one thing to remind a fellow believer of what God says in His Word and encourage them to repent and change their ways. It is another thing entirely to hold people outside the church to the same standards as believers. How can someone obey God's Word if they don't know what it says and don't have the Holy Spirit in their life to help them obey?

First Corinthians 5:12 says, "What business is it of mine to judge those outside the church? Are you not to judge those inside? God will judge those outside." In other words, don't worry about what people are doing outside of the church. It is not our job to condemn them. Calling them out in their sin is neither productive nor necessary. Instead, we can love on them. We can share the gospel with them. We can talk about what God has done in our lives and how we have been changed because of Christ. We can demonstrate our love for God through acts of kindness and compassion. We can pray for them and ask God to reveal Himself to them. We can even invite them to join us at church or in our small groups. But it is not our job to convict them. That is the Holy Spirit's job, and unless they give their lives to Christ, they are not going to be able to understand the full weight of their sin.

We have the ability to obey God's Word because we have the Holy Spirit in our lives to convict us. Even still, we will continue to fall short. Christians have a hard enough time as it is following God's Word. How can we expect someone who doesn't know Jesus and doesn't have the Holy Spirit in their lives to live up to the same standards? In 1 Corinthians 2:14, it says, "The person without the Spirit does not accept the things that come from the Spirit of God but considers them foolishness, and cannot understand them because they are discerned only through the Spirit." In other words, until someone has the Holy Spirit in their lives, they are going to be unable to discern what true wisdom is.

People change from the inside out, not the outside in. Telling nonbelievers that they need to change their behavior before they can become a Christian is setting people up to fail. It is also false doctrine. Romans 5:8 says, "God demonstrates his own love for us in this: *While we were still sinners*, Christ died for us." The Bible does not say that you need to clean up your act before you can become a Christian. It says that Christ died for us while we were still sinners; therefore, we can receive the free gift of grace at any point in our lives.

Once someone has accepted Jesus into their lives, we then have to trust that the Holy Spirit will reveal their sin to them and convict them to repent. For most people though, this isn't going to happen overnight. We can't expect new believers to know and understand all scripture the day they become a Christian. It is not as if we present new believers with a list of all their sins the day they accept Jesus into their lives. "Welcome to the club. Here are all the ways you are in violation of our rules. Guess we have to kick you out now."

There is often a transition period in which new believers are reconciling their new beliefs with their old ways of life. They may have to break off an unhealthy relationship, wean themselves off addictive behaviors, remove themselves from social situations that are too tempting for them, make new habits, form new relationships and join communities that are going to spurn them on toward righteousness, make changes to their finances, or work through areas in which they feel guilt and/or shame. This process can be incredibly painful and discouraging, and new believers need our compassion and our support during this transition, not our condemnation.

During this transition period, new believers are also learning God's Word and understanding the purpose of the Holy Spirit in their lives. Like Paul says in 1 Corinthians 3:1, they are still "mere infants in Christ." They are not ready for solid food yet but need to be fed with spiritual milk until they mature in Christ. Consequently, our job as fellow believers is to walk alongside our new brothers and sisters in Christ and disciple them (a.k.a. teach and train them) to understand what it means to be a follower of Christ. New believers need to learn how to walk with Christ before they can run.

Therefore, like any good teacher or coach, a discipler can't just tell a believer what they are doing wrong. Conversely, they shouldn't just tell a believer to do something because "the Bible says so." They should be able to explain why and should be able to role model what it looks like to be a mature follower of Christ.

OUR HANG-UPS WITH HYPOCRISY

This is another area in which Christians get confused. We live in an era that is hypersensitive to hypocrisy, which can make it extremely difficult for Christians to role model what it looks like to be a mature follower of Christ, especially since all Christians are still human and are bound to mess up from time to time. Some Christians role model a version of Christianity that is highly legalistic, whereas others role model a looser form of Christianity. We often don't know where to draw the line, and it can come across as very inconsistent or even hypocritical as Christians. If one believer says and does one thing and another believer says and does another thing, which one is right? At the end of the day, we are sending mixed messages, and people don't know how to sort through them.

For example, I recently had a friend who posted on her Instagram story a photo of a man holding up a sign that said, "according to the bible it is also a sin to get drunk or have tattoos but y'all drew the line at lgbtq people existing." In other words, why are Christians seemingly inconsistent in their understanding of what the Bible says is and is not a sin? To an outsider (and even some insiders), the line seems arbitrary. It can sometimes feel as if Christians have picked a handful of sins from the Bible that are really bad, while ignoring or minimizing the rest of them.

First of all, I think it is important to clarify that there are three types of laws provided by the Bible. The first set of laws were civil laws that constituted the civil government of the Israeli people in the Old Testament. These laws were designed for a specific group of people during a specific time in history that were intended to set the Jewish people apart from the neighboring cultures around them (e.g., circumcision, **?** food restrictions, tattoos, etc.). They were also intended to help the Jewish people strive for righteousness when they did not have the power of the Holy Spirit in their lives. These are the laws that we tend to disregard today because they were highly specific to a particular cultural context, and when Christ came to open up salvation for both the Jews and the Gentiles, these cultural distinctions became irrelevant. The Jews didn't need to distinguish themselves any longer from the Gentiles, because they were now all one in Christ.

The second set of laws were ceremonial laws (or Levitical Laws) that were a set of rules and regulations for how the Jewish people should make sacrifices to the Lord (e.g., how an animal should be prepared for a proper sacrifice). When Jesus died on the cross, paying the ultimate sacrifice for our sins, we no longer needed to make sacrifices because our debt had been paid in full. As a result, these ceremonial laws no longer were required, not because of history, culture, and time but because of theology. No more blood needed to be shed, because the blood of Christ was more than enough to reconcile us to God. Sacrificial ceremonies and rituals became meaningless because no human act could do what Jesus had already done. Therefore, even though we don't follow these laws today, they are an important reminder of how impossible it was to please God without the perfect sacrifice of His Son.

Whereas the first two sets of laws were abolished and fulfilled through the life and death of Jesus Christ, the third set of laws are the ones we still uphold as Christians today. This third set of laws are moral laws, which are centered around the Ten Commandments as well as other commands in the Old Testament that were reflective of God's character and holiness. Most of these moral laws have been reinforced by the New Testament through the teachings of Jesus Christ.

In many ways, however, Jesus took these moral laws from the Old Testament and went one step further. For example, in Matthew 5:21–22, Jesus says, "You have heard that it was said to the people long ago, 'Do not murder, and anyone who murders will be subject to judgment.' But I tell you that anyone who is angry with his brother will be subject to judgment." What Jesus often reiterated through His teachings was that it is not just about the letter of the law, it is about the spirit of the law. In other words, it is our hearts that matter when we stand before God, not just our actions.

This point is important for moving forward. Whereas the Pharisees had an extremely legalistic standard of the law that they imposed on their followers, Jesus stood in stark contrast to this legalism, not to say that pursuing righteousness isn't a holy pursuit but to say that how we pursue righteousness is just as important as the end result. Whereas the world judges based on the outside, the Lord judges based on the inside.

What this means is that there is a difference between the moral laws outlined in scripture that we must uphold and the guidelines that are either self-imposed or recommended by the church or fellow believers as ways to help honor and uphold the moral laws outlined in scripture. In other words, we may all share the same goal of pursuing righteousness, but how we get there may look different for each person, depending on where their heart is at with the Lord. First Corinthians 10:23 tells us that even though we may have the right to do something, that doesn't mean it is beneficial. That means, as Christians, we must exercise discernment and go beyond just the letter of the law when making wise choices. Holiness isn't just a checklist of rules that you must follow but is a reflection of our hearts.

For example, my husband and I do not spend one-on-one time with individuals of the opposite sex unless they are a relative or a work colleague for a necessary work-related meeting or task. This guideline is not outlined in scripture and is not considered a moral law that we must uphold. Nevertheless, my husband and I want to honor our marriage and keep our relationship pure, and so we choose to not put ourselves in situations that could become a temptation in the future.

Have we on occasion broken our own guideline? Totally. There have been situations that have come up that we both agreed were harmless or unavoidable, and we did not want to be legalistic; however, most of the time, we seek to honor this guideline out of respect for each other and our marriage. Although I trust my husband and my husband trusts me, we understand that we are still susceptible to temptation, no matter how strong of Christians we are. We would both rather play it safe and not even allow Satan the opportunity to try to put a wedge in between us. The Bible tells us to *flee* sexual immorality, not just to avoid it. Additionally, it tells us that even impure thoughts are considered adultery, not just the physical or emotional act of cheating on your spouse. Therefore, this guideline is a reflection of our hunger and thirst for righteousness in our marriage.

Now, would I recommend this guideline to other Christian married couples? Absolutely. If you really want to flee sexual immorality and strive for righteousness in your marriage, I think this is a helpful *guideline* to add to your toolkit. The heart behind this guideline is a reflection of my husband's and my desire to uphold the moral laws outlined in scripture.

However, as much as I would recommend this guideline for other Christian couples, it is not my job to impose my convictions on other believers. In other words, I can recommend practices that have worked well for me, but I cannot condemn other believers for not following my own self-imposed guidelines. It is not my place to judge the convictions other Christians might have regarding how they interact with people of the opposite sex. Some Christians might be stricter in their convictions, and others might be more relaxed, even though we all share the same end goal of purity.

Therefore, we can make recommendations. We can explain our heart behind why we have personally made a decision. We can encourage certain behaviors that have worked for us. We can remind our fellow believers that the spirit of the law is just as important as the letter of the law. However, we are not able to see the inward workings of someone's heart. We do not know or understand the struggles and temptations someone may face, or the ways that someone has been personally convicted by the Holy Spirit.

For example, for someone who struggles with drunkenness, it might make sense for them to avoid drinking altogether. If one drink is too tempting, then it is best that they stay sober. But for someone who doesn't struggle with drunkenness, having a drink or two is not going to lead to the same temptation. It is perfectly OK if one believer feels convicted to never drink and the other believer is OK with drinking, as long as it is in moderation.

It is human nature though to cast judgment on the convictions of others. It would be all too easy for the person who feels convicted to never drink to judge their fellow believer for having a drink. On the other hand, it would also be easy for the person who is able to have a drink without feeling tempted to think that the individual who never drinks is being too legalistic.

Thus, there is the moral law in all its formality, and then there is the practicality of the law that results in a set of personal or communal guidelines that are helpful for pursuing righteousness on a daily basis. The problem is when these guidelines get treated as the moral law themselves, imposing a legality on individuals that is neither helpful nor warranted.

The reality is we are all trying to work through on an individual basis what it means to be a Christian. We all have the same end goal, but we all have to figure out the best way to achieve that goal without stumbling in the process. Our relationship with God is unique and personal, and the ways God will reveal Himself will look differently with each person. That being said, we have been given scripture as a road map and the life of Jesus Christ as an example to follow. If we truly desire to pursue righteousness, we should be utilizing every resource at our disposal, including one another as brothers and sisters in Christ. Not only should you be prepared to walk alongside a fellow believer, you should also be ready and willing to have a fellow believer walk alongside you. We are all in this together, even though our individual paths might all look different.

At the end of the day, we serve a God who has given us all grace, even though we do not deserve it. This truth should prompt us all to bestow the same grace on others that has been given to us. When we channel a heart of humility and gratitude, we find ourselves more concerned about our own shortcomings than the shortcomings of others. Therefore, as Christians, our primary message should first and foremost be the gospel and the ways God has transformed our *own* lives. Through the power of the Holy Spirit, we can then trust that when we are actually living out our faith and demonstrating God's love and grace, people will naturally be drawn to Christ. There is no sin too big, no heart too hard, no obstacle too difficult for Jesus to overcome, so we need to stop limiting the power of God to our own self-imposed standards.

CHAPTER 6
GOD IS THE KING OF SOCIAL JUSTICE

'Cause when You speak, and when You move
When You do what only You can do
It changes us
It changes what we see and what we seek

—"Spirit of the Living God" by Vertical Worship

When I was in high school, there was a teacher named Mrs. Jones who was arguably the most influential teacher on our campus. She was an English teacher, but her true passion was social justice causes, and she had a gift for teaching students about how to have compassion and be an advocate for the oppressed, the underrepresented, the marginalized. In my tenth-grade English class, we did a project on genocide that to this day is one of the most influential projects I have ever done. It sparked in me a passion for international justice causes, which led me to pursue a degree in political science with an emphasis in international relations. I now have a PhD in the subject, and my research interests are still on civil conflicts, particularly ethnic and religious civil conflicts.

That tenth-grade English project impacted the trajectory of my entire career. Not only did Mrs. Jones open our eyes to social justice causes, but she also encouraged us and gave us opportunities to do something about it. I later took her social justice class in which we got to work on social justice projects that we were passionate about. Through that class, I became copresident of a club on campus called STAND (Students Taking Action Now: Darfur) in which we raised awareness of the genocide taking place in Sudan and raised money for relief efforts. It was definitely one of the most powerful experiences of my high school career, thanks to Mrs. Jones.

Through the classes she taught, the clubs she sponsored, and the events and fundraisers she planned, Mrs. Jones became a social justice icon on our campus. Everyone knew what she was about and admired and respected her passion and compassion. She almost even had a cult following of young high schoolers who wanted to be just like her.

However, as much as I appreciate Mrs. Jones's impact on my life and all that she taught me, to this day it makes me incredibly sad when I think about her because I know that she was not a believer. She is someone who cared so much about helping others and wanted desperately for her life to be meaningful, but she did not love Jesus. I haven't seen Mrs. Jones in more than ten years, but I wonder how she is doing today. I can't imagine how discouraging it must feel over time to spend your whole life putting your hope in this world, only to watch it disappoint. There is always a new war, a new genocide, a new group of marginalized people, a new natural disaster, a new economic crisis, a new form of hate speech ... the list goes on and on. As someone who studies politics and the world for a living, I am so thankful that my hope is not in this world and that I can rest assured in the fact that one day the world will actually be a better place, in fact a perfect place, when Jesus returns.

At the end of the day, however, the most renowned teacher on campus, known for their love, compassion, and commitment to social justice, was not a Christian. Talk about making us look bad! In John 13:34–35, Jesus says, "A new command I give you: Love one another. As I have loved you, so you must love one another. By this everyone will know that you are my disciples, if you love one another." In other words, taken from a popular Christian hymn, "They will know we are Christians by our love." It is, therefore, incredibly confusing when some of the nicest, most loving people you know are not Christians. I often think about how many high school students have gone through my high school and have graduated thinking that their non-Christian teachers were more influential to their development than their Christian teachers.

This is not meant to be a guilt trip for Christians, and I am not trying to make everyone feel bad about letting nonbelievers beat us at our own game. I am, however, trying to call our attention to a major issue that is creating a lot of confusion in the world today. I actually know many people, millennials in particular, who have walked away from the church because they felt that Christians were not doing a good enough job championing the causes of the weak, the poor, the destitute, the marginalized. In their minds, Christians were not practicing what they were preaching and were majorly falling short when it came to meeting the needs of the less fortunate. It has only become more obvious that you don't need to be a Christian to be a good person, and there are a lot of great people out there, like Mrs. Jones, who are not believers.

However, there is a major difference between having social justice as your ultimate mission and having the gospel as your ultimate mission. In the former, social justice is the end goal, whereas in the latter, social justice is a means to a different end goal, which is sharing the good news of Christ and enacting God's kingdom here on earth. Social justice for social justice's sake is meaningless if the gospel is not at the heart of it. This may sound blunt, but food, water, shelter, freedom, equality, justice, and world peace do not save your soul. Social justice is a noble cause and is something that Jesus cares deeply about, but even something that is well intentioned and inherently good can still become an idol when it is elevated above Christ.

There are essentially two ends of the spectrum here, and neither end is good. On the one side, you have people who claim to be Christians who are doing nothing to help the poor or oppressed and are living in their safe little Christian bubbles, surrounded by like-minded people who share the same privileges as them. They are neither aware of the needs of others nor proactive in sharing the love of Christ through both their words and deeds. They might give a portion of their money away at a distance but are never willing to get close to the people who need the love of Jesus the most. They claim Jesus, but they are not willing to get dirty or mess up their own perfect lives for the sake of the gospel.

Now on the other side, you have the opposite extreme. There you have people who are not believers and are oftentimes adamantly opposed to Christianity. However, they are organizing fundraisers, participating in marches and protests, lobbying politicians, volunteering at homeless shelters and soup kitchens, all in the name of social justice. They can be some of the nicest and most selfless people you know. The problem is that even though they are able to recognize the brokenness of the world and want to do something about it, they are only treating the symptoms of the disease rather than the disease itself. They will offer people food, money, shelter, health care, freedom, and political representation, but they will never give people what they need the most, hope in Jesus and the salvation of their souls. On the outside, it may look like they are outperforming others in their love and compassion for the world. However, if a doctor were to only treat a patient's symptoms of the disease rather than the disease itself, they would be sued for malpractice. Therefore, we should not allow ourselves to be deceived by nice-sounding cures that only lead to earthly consolation, rather than spiritual healing and redemption.

That being said, a good doctor first treats the disease itself, but is also empathetic to the fact that the symptoms of the disease are also painful. No one wants a doctor who has a horrible bedside manner and leaves you in discomfort and pain while they exclusively treat the root cause of the disease. Over time, they would start to lose their credibility as a healer. Ideally a good doctor would try to cure you while also trying to alleviate your symptoms as well. Similarly, as Christians, we must first seek to offer spiritual healing, but in doing so, we should also be empathetic to the fact that we are all suffering the earthly consequences of the Fall, and those consequences are also painful. Our credibility as believers is often jeopardized when we fail to acknowledge injustice as a major (and extremely painful) symptom of our collective sin natures.

FAITH WITHOUT WORKS IS DEAD

So then, what should social justice look like for believers? In James 2:17 (ESV), it tells us that "faith without works is dead." Therefore, if you truly love Jesus and have the Holy Spirit in your life, you should be compelled to action. You will begin to see people through the eyes of Jesus; your heart will break for the things Jesus's heart breaks for. Your life will be an outpouring of the Holy Spirit through love, joy, peace, patience, kindness, goodness, faithfulness, gentleness, and self-control. You won't want to sit on the sidelines; injustice will make your blood boil with righteous anger. The brokenness of the world will bring you to your knees in prayer.

In fact, social justice should be at the core of the gospel. The fact that the world is riddled with hate, injustice, inequality, corruption, oppression, deceit, poverty, and sorrow is a glaring reminder of our personal and collective need of a savior. It is a physical manifestation of how out of control the consequences of sin are. Our deep desire to see all things made new is intimately connected to our longing for Jesus Christ. If we turn a blind eye to the ways in which the world is broken, we are essentially denying the power of Christ to transform ourselves and our world.

We are even told in scripture that the two greatest commandments are to "Love the Lord your God" and "Love your neighbor as yourself." First John 3:17–18 (ESV) also says, "But if anyone has the world's goods and sees his brother in need, yet closes his heart against him, how does God's love abide in him? Little children, let us not love in word or talk but in deed and in truth." Are we putting our money where our mouth is? Are we generous with both our time and our resources? Are we living out the gospel in both our words and actions? Are we denying ourselves and our rights to put the needs of others ahead of us? Do we love God so much that we want to be the hands and feet of Jesus to bring the love of Christ to our communities?

The unfortunate reality is that for many Christians, the answer is no. Many Christians prefer the comforts of their own little bubbles and rarely venture out into the spaces that need Christ's love the most. Love requires sacrifice, and we are by nature selfish creatures. It is easy to become complacent and distracted by our own wants and desires that we never look beyond ourselves. Motivated by our own comfort and well-being, we are often willing to accept the status quo, even if it continues to hurt others, in order to not have to take any risks or put ourselves out there. And to be honest, I think we can all relate to this at times. I myself feel convicted of this on a regular basis, and it is indeed something that the church needs to constantly address. Comfort and complacency are weapons of the enemy, utilized to suppress the full manifestation of the Holy Spirit in the lives of believers. Therefore, we must all be on guard in order to not let our own sin natures get in the way of sharing the love of Christ with our communities.

It is also important to recognize, however, that there are also people who claim Jesus out there whose lives have not been transformed by the gospel. This can be confusing to people who don't understand that not all people who claim to be Christians are actually followers of Christ. In fact, the news loves to report stories about "Christians" who are on the side of injustice. We can unfortunately all think of numerous stories in which "Christians" are being racist, sexist, selfish, or hateful. However, just because something is done in the name of Christianity does not mean that it is from Christ, and just because someone claims to be a Christian does not mean that they are true followers of Jesus. Therefore, we all need to be wary of wolves in sheep's clothing who are puppets of the enemy in his never-ending quest to undermine and discredit the work of true believers.

That being said, the good news is that there are many Christians out there who are getting it right, even though these stories don't make front-page news. In fact, research studies have consistently shown that people in the church as a whole are far more generous with their time and money than people outside of the church. For example, in a recent study conducted by the University of Indiana's School of Philanthropy, individuals with a religious affiliation are more than *over* two times more likely to donate to charity than those without a religious affiliation.[38] In addition, this study showed that frequently attending religious services and being connected to a religious community amplified giving rates even more.[39]

Furthermore, this study utilized a very narrow definition of giving, which excluded giving to faith-based nonprofits. Other studies that utilize a more expansive definition of giving estimate that "faith motivates as much as *75 percent* of all charity in the United States."[40] According to the PEW Research Center, "highly religious individuals," defined as individuals who pray daily and attend religious services at least once a week, are approximately 60 percent more likely to have volunteered in the last week and approximately 60 percent more likely to have donated time, money, and goods to the poor in the last week.[41]

---

[38] Bradford Richardson, "Religious people more likely to give to charity, study shows," *The Washington Times,* October 30, 2017, https://www.washingtontimes.com/news/2017/oct/30/religious-people-more-likely-give-charity-study

[39] Bradford Richardson, "Religious people more likely to give to charity, study shows."

[40] Bradford Richardson, "Religious people more likely to give to charity, study shows."

[41] "Religion in Everyday Life," *PEW Research Center,* April 12, 2016, https://www.pewforum.org/2016/04/12/religion-in-everyday-life/

Therefore, contrary to popular opinion, the world's most generous individuals are often the ones who are deeply committed to their faith. Can you even imagine what the world would look like if you took away all the time, money, and resources Christians devoted to making the world a better place? I think this is important to address, because we live in a world that likes to portray Christians as selfish, miserly, and hypocritical; however, I think that is not entirely a fair assessment. Yes, the church could be doing better, and all of us Christians could step up our game, but the reality is there are a lot of churches and people within the church who are getting it right. They are loving their communities and stepping up to fulfill needs that no one else is willing or able to fill. Just because their work has gone unnoticed or unpublicized does not mean it is not taking place.

I only say this as a response to the many conversations I have had with nonbelievers or people who have walked away from the church, who use Christian complacency as their main argument for why they don't believe in God or why they no longer associate with the church (even though ironically many of them are also not actively volunteering their time, money, or resources themselves). In their minds, Christians are sitting back and doing nothing, when in reality they just aren't aware of what many of the Christians are doing in their life. Again, just because the work of believers is not being publicized does not mean that it is not happening. In addition, these statistics don't even begin to capture the countless hours Christians have spent sharing the gospel in their communities, ministering to the spiritual needs of people, not just their physical needs. If we truly believe that what people really need is Jesus, then our work should look much different than that of our nonbeliever peers.

In fact, scripture even tells us that many of our good works as believers should be done in secret. Matthew 6:1–4 says, "Be careful not to practice your righteousness in front of others to be seen by them. If you do, you will have no reward from your Father in heaven. So when you give to the needy, do not announce it with trumpets, as the hypocrites do in the synagogues and on the streets, to be honored by others. Truly I tell you, they have received their reward in full. But when you give to the needy, do not let your left hand know what your right hand is doing, so that your giving may be in secret. Then your Father, who sees what is done in secret, will reward you."

I think these verses are especially pertinent in the age of social media. Our commitment to social justice should go beyond what we post on our social media sites. Our generosity should not be prompted by the potential of a photo op. Whereas the world may judge us off of how we present ourselves on our social media platforms and draw conclusions about our hearts based on what we do or do not post, God judges us based on what we do when no one is watching. For example, it has become incredibly popular to be seen as a social justice activist on social media, especially in an election year; however, for a majority of people, this commitment to social justice causes is purely virtual. It does not match up with a lifestyle of self-sacrifice, and interest in these issues wane when an election is over or an issue is no longer trending on social media. Although our social media platforms can indeed be a platform for good, social media engagement should not be confused for the real, hands-on, time-consuming work of Christ.

At the end of the day, the work of a true believer is often done behind the scenes and out of the spotlight. It is often not glamourous or flashy, and we may never get credit for the work we do. However, just because our commitment to social justice doesn't make front-page news does not mean that our social justice work doesn't matter. Our heavenly Father sees how we are treating people in our communities, and we will be judged for our selflessness and love for others. In Matthew 25, Jesus says that he will separate the sheep from the goats based on how they treated the least of these in society. As a result, there will be many people who will be surprised by their judgment. They will say, "Lord, when did we see you hungry or thirsty or a stranger or needing clothes or sick or in prison, and did not help you?'" and He will reply, "Truly I tell you, whatever you did not do for one of the least of these, you did not do for me" (Matthew 25:44–45).

These passages should scare us a little. All throughout scripture, it is overwhelmingly clear that being a true believer of Christ requires us to lay down our life and our rights for the sake of the gospel. It is not that our good works save us, but if we claim to love Jesus, and our actions do not reflect that, then we are in desperate need of a wake-up call. Our lip service to the mission of Jesus is not enough. Being fully transformed by the gospel should turn our lives upside down, and as a result, our lives should be producing spiritual fruit and an outpouring of the Holy Spirit. Social justice is, therefore, inherent to the gospel of Christ, and a commitment to social justice should be a natural response of a true believer.

HOWEVER, GOOD WORKS FOR GOOD WORKS' SAKE IS NOT ENOUGH

It is evidently clear from scripture that faith without works is dead. And yet it is also important for us believers to remember that the main purpose of our good works and being generous with our time, money, privilege, and resources is to bring glory to God. It is not enough as Christians to just be a good person or to be perceived as being generous or as social justice activists by our peers and communities. Matthew 5:16 (ESV) tells us to "let your light shine before others, *so that* they may see your good works and give glory to your Father who is in heaven" (emphasis added). I cannot underscore this enough. Our good works are designed to direct people to Jesus. Good works for good works' sake is not enough. If our good works are not pointing people to Jesus, then what is the point?

My husband and I used to do high school ministry, and one of the questions we would often ask our students is what they were doing to share the gospel on their campuses. A lot of students would say that they just tried to be a really nice person, in hopes that one day someone would ask them about their faith. I would then ask them, How would someone know to ask you about your faith if they don't even know that you are a Christian? They usually didn't have an answer for that, and I am guessing that most of you, and myself included, have never had someone just randomly come up to you to say, "Hey, I have noticed that you are a super nice person. Can you tell me about Jesus?" As previously discussed, there are a lot of nice people in the world doing nice things. Not all of them love Jesus. How then would an outsider be able to distinguish between a Christian nice person and a non-Christian nice person?

I am sure that many of you have heard the saying "preach the gospel; if necessary, use words." I have actually heard many people say that this is one of their favorite quotes. It is usually attributed to St. Francis of Assisi; however, what most people don't know is that St. Francis never actually said anything like it.[42] St. Francis did tell his followers to practice what they preach, but this quote has totally been taken out of context and has taken on a life of its own. It sounds good on a bumper sticker, but it is not scripturally accurate. There is nowhere in the Bible that says that we should avoid using words to preach the gospel. We just need to look to Jesus as our example. Jesus did countless miracles. He healed the sick, gave sight to the blind, reached out to the marginalized in society, and cared for the poor, but He always told them to repent and to turn toward God in doing so.

For Jesus, performing miracles and doing good works was a vessel for His main objective, saving humankind. Jesus did not come down to earth just to do a couple of cool tricks and help out a few people. He came to abolish sin, conquer death, and offer eternal hope and redemption to a fallen world. His miracles and good works were signs of His love and power, but at the end of the day, they were designed to point people to their need for a savior.

Although Jesus fulfilled many physical needs for people, He cared more about their spiritual needs. In John 6:35, Jesus says, "I am the bread of life. Whoever comes to me will never go hungry, and whoever believes in me will never be thirsty." Jesus wasn't saying that if you turn toward Jesus, you will have a lifetime supply of food and beverages. He was saying that at the end of the day, all you need is Jesus, and He will fill and sustain you with eternal life.

When Jesus healed the paralytic man in Luke 5 (ESV), he simply told the man, "Friend, your sins are forgiven." He didn't even acknowledge the fact that the man was now able to walk, because it was more important that the man's sins were forgiven. Not surprisingly, this infuriated the Pharisees, because who is able to forgive sins, except God himself? Jesus responded to the Pharisees by saying, "Which is easier: to say, 'Your sins are forgiven,' or to say, 'Get up and walk?' *But that you may know* that the Son of Man has authority on the earth to forgive sins" (emphasis added). He said to the paralytic, "I tell you, get up, pick up your mat, and go home." In other words, the physical healing of the paralytic was only meant to demonstrate

---

[42] Michael A. Milton, "What Does it Mean to "Use Words Only if Necessary" When Sharing the Gospel?" *Christianity.com* https://www.christianity.com/wiki/church/what-does-it-mean-to-use-words-only-if-necessary-when-sharing-the-gospel.html

God's power and authority. It was merely a symbol of the spiritual healing ?
that Jesus came down to give.

In response to all that took place, in Luke 5:25–26 (ESV), it goes on
to say that "immediately the man stood up before them, took what he
had been lying on, and went home glorifying God. Everyone was taken
with amazement and glorified God." Again, the purpose of the healing
was to bring glory to God. What I think is amazing about all this was
that everyone's immediate reaction was to praise and glorify God, not
even Jesus, who was the one they saw perform the miracle. At this time,
people didn't fully realize that Jesus was God incarnate, but they knew here
that the power Jesus displayed was from God and that God was the one
working through this man whom they had just met. They could have been
enamored with Jesus's "cool trick," but instead their immediate reaction
was to worship God.

Let me bring this all back to social justice in the world today. Social
justice is important, and Christians should be actively engaged in social
justice missions. Christians should be championing the marginalized,
meeting the needs of the poor, tearing down systems of oppression, and
laying down their rights and privilege to serve the "least of these." They
should be sharing their money and resources, sacrificing their time and
comfort, getting out of their Christian bubbles to engage with people
who are different from them, spending time in prayer, and even risking
their lives. However, in doing all this, they should first and foremost be
proclaiming the good news of Jesus. Their actions should be spreading
eternal hope, not just earthly hope. They should be meeting people's
spiritual needs, not just their physical needs.

It is, therefore, incredibly important for Christians to not fall prey to
messages that sound nice but are only halfway rooted in truth. Colossians
2:8 says, "See to it that no one takes you captive through hollow and
deceptive philosophy, which depends on human tradition and the
elemental spiritual forces of this world rather than on Christ." It is so easy
to be consumed by causes that are indeed noble and sound good but are
forgetting the most important point.

For example, I know many people, on both ends of the political
spectrum, who are so passionate about a particular cause or issue that they
are not afraid to speak up, put themselves out there, risk being criticized,

or endanger their reputation. However, that same valiance is noticeably absent when it comes to proclaiming or defending their faith. It is socially acceptable, in America at least, to speak out on particular political or social issues. Particularly in the age of social media, it is seen as heroic or noble to champion particular causes, even if it is just from the comfort of your couch.

It is no longer acceptable, however, to advocate for your religious beliefs. Say all you want about health care, welfare policies, prison reform, and racial inequality, but keep religion out of it. You can be an activist but not an evangelist. As a result, Christians often fall silent on key issues out of fear of sounding politically incorrect, or they just imitate the rhetoric of nonbelievers to blend in and sound like they are on the right side of justice. They may talk a big talk, but they don't walk a big walk.

If we truly believe in the power of the gospel and that Jesus has the power to change hearts and overturn systems of injustice, why don't we act like we do? Instead of retweeting what politicians, activists, or celebrities are saying on an issue, why don't we share what God says on an issue? If we truly believe in the power of prayer, why aren't we constantly on our knees in prayer asking God to radically transform our world, our nation, our government, and our leaders? If our goal is truly to become more like Jesus, why aren't we out in our communities spending time with the least of these, sharing the love and hope of Christ?

When it comes to issues of social justice, we have a cure that is far beyond any of the solutions of this world. Revelation 21:4–5 tells us that one day God "will wipe every tear from their eyes. There will be no more death or mourning or crying or pain, for the old order of things has passed away." He will make all things new. How amazing is that! We serve a God who is the king of social justice. He is going to right every wrong and take care of every injustice in the world. There will be no more unfairness or inequality. Evil will be vanquished, and love will win. He will do what centuries of humans have unsuccessfully tried to do.

In the meantime, though, it is our job as believers to give people a taste of heaven here on earth. Although no one can truly fathom what the kingdom of heaven will be like, we can give people a glimpse of what it could be like. When the world sees Christians actively fighting for things like peace, justice, reconciliation, and human dignity, we are not only able to communicate that these are issues that God cares about, but we can remind people that our hope is not in this world but in a redeemed version of this world. Earthly freedom and peace are merely a shadow of the eternal freedom and peace we will experience in heaven.

However, a shadow can be really convincing evidence that the real thing exists.

CHAPTER 7
WHO WOULD JESUS VOTE FOR?

You have no rival, You have no equal
Now and forever, Our God reigns
Yours is the Kingdom, Yours is the glory
Yours is the Name, above all names
What a powerful Name it is
What a powerful Name it is
The Name of Jesus Christ my King

—"What a Beautiful Name" by Hillsong Worship

Mentions this repeatedly.

I avoided writing this chapter for a long time because I know that politics is an extremely sensitive topic and I don't want anyone to think that I am pushing a particular political agenda. I also have a PhD in political science, and somehow that makes it feel like there is more pressure on this chapter, that people are craving to hear a magical solution to the tense political climate that we live in, and that I need to deliver in a big way. Also, this is the chapter that inspired me to write this book in the first place, and as a result, I have a deep personal connection to the ideas that I am about to express. In many ways, I feel like I have been writing this chapter for years in my mind and I am excited to finally see these thoughts come to life.

Let me start at the beginning. I grew up in a Christian home in a California suburb just outside of Sacramento. My dad was a middle school principal and my mom an elementary school teacher in a large public school district in Elk Grove, California. For a few years, Elk Grove was the fastest-growing city in America, and my high school was in the top 5 percent of the most ethnically diverse high schools in the US. It actually wasn't until I went to college at Cal Poly San Luis Obispo that I even realized that the United States was actually still a majority white. I literally almost fell out of my chair when my professor brought up that statistic. I had been one of only a handful of blonde girls in my high school of almost three thousand and had grown accustomed to being surrounded by people of different races, ethnicities, cultural backgrounds, religions, socioeconomic statuses, and political beliefs. I was used to interacting with people who looked different from me, thought differently than I did, and believed different things than I did.

When it came to politics, my parents were not particularly vocal about their political beliefs and identified more as Independents than anything. Influenced by both their church upbringings and their experiences as public school educators in California, they straddled the political line and had fairly moderate perspectives on politics. Like most American teenagers, I absorbed many of the political beliefs of my parents at an early age. My parents were smart, wise, reasonable people, and I decided that I agreed with many of their political viewpoints.

When it came to the 2008 presidential election, I was one of the lucky few students in my class who turned eighteen in time to vote (yay for October birthdays!). I, like most millennials, was enamored with Barack Obama, who represented a new era of politicians. At my high school, it seemed like everyone was equally obsessed with Obama, and I experienced very little resistance to my political beliefs.

However, one day I was at a coffee shop with some people from church and I said offhand that I voted for Obama. Almost immediately, one of my high school youth leaders jumped in and told me that I could not be a Christian if I voted for a Democrat. I was honestly stunned. What do you mean I couldn't be a Christian? Even at a young age, I took my faith very seriously and was deeply committed to my religious beliefs. Weren't politics a totally separate issue? Didn't we settle the church versus state debate a long time ago and decide that it was best if they remained separate?

This was the first time I had experienced outright hostility for my political beliefs, and it was from a mentor figure from my church whom I had trusted and respected. I was hurt. I was outraged. I was confused. For an eighteen-year-old, I actually knew my Bible really well, and I was fairly certain that the Bible didn't say anything about how we should vote or who we should vote for. In fact, the passages I remembered from scripture all seemed to make it clear that our citizenship was in heaven and that we were to focus our attention on eternity, rather than on the things of this world.

For the next ten years, I wrestled with this question of faith and politics. I came to realize that my high school youth leader wasn't the only Christian who was adamantly opposed to anything associated with the Democratic Party. In fact, most Christians, across most of the United States, tended to vote Republican, and the Republican Party was often revered by Christians as the antidote to our God-forsaken country.

Although I did not, and still do not, identify as a strong Democrat (I actually identify myself as a Centrist and strongly dislike both political parties), I found that in most Christian circles, I was often perceived as being super liberal. I found myself arguing for the Democratic Party, not because I was married to their political perspective or policy preferences but because I felt like I needed to be a counterweight to the strong right pull among my fellow believers. I felt like my fellow believers were so enamored with the Republican Party that if the Republican Party told them to jump off a cliff, they would. I, therefore, felt like the lone Christian metaphorically screaming at the top of their lungs, "Don't jump!" as I watched members of my Christian community fall into the political abyss.

Fast-forward to 2016. In the midst of a brutal campaign year, the topic of who are you going to vote for was at an astronomical high. The Trump versus Clinton deathmatch brought even the most apathetic of voters curiously to the sidelines. As exciting as this election was to watch, many people seemed to be in inner turmoil over their vote decision. Often described as picking the "lesser of two evils," the average citizen seemed to be weighing their decision far more than usual.

As a Christian, I saw this inner turmoil amplified even further among Christian voters. Traditionally, Christians tend to vote for the Republican candidate because the Republican Party is often perceived as being more in alignment with Christian values. However, to have a presidential candidate who was unfathomably far from the Christian ideal, it was easy to see why Christians were particularly unsettled by their decision. I know many

Christians who felt like no matter who they chose, they were going to be sinning by their vote.

Despite this inner turmoil many Christian voters faced in the 2016 election, a decisive majority of 79 percent of evangelical Christians voted for Donald Trump, along with a substantial majority of 59 percent of nonevangelical, born-again Christians.[43] As a political scientist, I was in no way surprised by these statistics, given the fact that Christians have been married to the Republican Party now for several decades. In addition, political scientists now claim that religion, not race, is the single biggest predictor of vote choice in America.[44]

The problem was the ways in which Donald Trump was fervently endorsed by the Christian community both before and after the election sent a very confusing message to the rest of the world about what Christians stand for. Although I believe that most Christians were well intentioned and had some very legitimate policy concerns that were driving their vote choice, the desire to win the election created an incentive to turn a blind eye to the ways in which Trump was not aligned with Christian values. Christians were willing to stay silent on some issues so that other issues could take precedent. Although often justified under the guise of making sacrifices for the greater good, in many ways, what Christians unintentionally communicated to the rest of the world is that God is more interested in enacting a party platform than His perfect plan for creation.

At the same time, Christians who were Democrats were not immune to this same issue. Even though there were significantly fewer Christians who voted Democrat in the 2016 election, I know many believers who were also willing to turn a blind eye to the ways that Hillary Clinton and the Democratic Party were not aligned with Christian values so that they could win the election. They too were willing to make excuses for their team and were unwilling to call out their own leaders.

All in all, the real result of the 2016 election was a multitude of Christians who cowardly stayed silent on many issues of injustice that God cares about so that their political candidate would win. Christians

---

[43] "Notional Christians: The Big Election Story in 2016," *Barna Research Group,* December 1, 2016, https://www.barna.com/research/notional-christians-big-election-story-2016/

[44] "How to forecast an American's vote," *The Economist,* November 3, 2018, https://www.economist.com/graphic-detail/2018/11/03/how-to-forecast-an-americans-vote

were more concerned about justifying their vote choice and the actions of their political party than speaking up for truth on *all* fronts. They were over eager in criticizing the shortcomings of the opposing political party but unwilling to hold their own leaders to the same standards. Blinded by their own false sense of self-righteousness, believers were not willing to admit the ways that they were willing to compromise on their beliefs.

Moreover, I honestly can't help but be very disappointed in American Christians today. I am convinced that if Jesus were on this earth today, "Who would you vote for?" would be one of those questions that the Pharisees would ask to try to trap Jesus. The sad thing is I think most Christians today would assume that Jesus would clearly choose the Republican candidate. On the other hand, there is even a growing population in the United States that would adamantly argue that Jesus is a Democrat. These two groups of people would then fight tooth and nail trying to convince the other that Jesus would be on their team.

However, the very thought of calling Jesus a Republican or a Democrat makes me cringe. To ascribe Jesus an earthly identity and to put Him in a box created by humankind seems blasphemous. And yet, whether we realize it or not, we do this all the time. Instead of asking how Jesus fits into our politics, maybe instead we should be asking, How do our politics fit in with our understanding of Jesus? It's like when the stepsisters in *Cinderella* are trying to convince the prince and his advisors that the glass slipper fits their foot when clearly they do not go together. We can keep trying to squeeze the glass slipper on our foot until it fits, but no matter how hard we try, it is only going to result in disaster. In other words, we can try to keep forcing our religious beliefs into our pre-set political ideologies, but our beliefs as Christians are much bigger than our political ideologies and no matter how hard we try, these two things do not perfectly fit together. Scripture was not intended to be cherry-picked to justify a worldly political platform. Instead, we should be setting our sights on God's plan for creation and critically examining how the things of the world line up (or do not line up) with scripture, not the other way around.

Therefore, in this chapter, I want to take a step back to try to look at things from God's perspective. Before proceeding though, I want everyone to try to remove themselves from their existing partisan loyalties and to check their political biases. We all have them, so be honest with yourself about the ways in which our perspectives have been influenced by the environments we live in. We are all a product of our family backgrounds, the communities we live in, our race, gender, education, socioeconomic status, religious denomination, and so on. All these things influence how we view the world and are sometimes even in competition with one another. However, if we want to shift our perspective to be more in alignment with Christ, we need to take a step back and reprogram our brains to eliminate the influence of worldly thinking in our lives.

WHAT DOES THE BIBLE SAY ABOUT POLITICS?

Moving forward, I want to begin by taking a look at some of the things the Bible says about politics to give us all a foundation to build off of. Probably the most well-known passage in scripture related to politics is the traditional "Give back to Caesar what is Caesar's and to God what is God's" in Mark 12:17. This is a reminder that our "citizenship" (Philippians 3:20) is not here on earth but is in heaven. We are just passing through this world and serve as ambassadors for Christ. Although we are called to follow the rules of the land and to pay homage to the ruling powers, Jesus makes a very clear distinction between things of this world versus things of heaven. Second Corinthians 4:18 states, "So we fix our eyes not on what is seen, but on what is unseen, since what is seen is temporary, but what is unseen is eternal." As we push on toward the eternal, we are not to put our hope in this world or in things of this world, because the things of this world are temporary and will pass away.

Psalm 146:3 also states, "Do not put your trust in princes, in human beings, who cannot save." Or in modern-day language since we no longer have princes (at least in America), "Do not put your trust in presidents, senators, governors, and so on, who are all just human beings who cannot save." So why do we continue to look to our political leaders of this world to champion the causes of Christ? When Jesus came down to this earth, He could have easily chosen to hold a position of power, but He didn't. Jesus was a carpenter—not a politician, a king, or a warrior—so why do we hold positions of power with such esteem when Jesus Himself rejected all forms of earthy power, taking on the form of a servant to direct people to His Father in heaven?

In the book of 1 Samuel, the prophet Samuel is about to pass away, and the Jews beg for him to appoint a king, like the nations surrounding them, to lead them once he is gone. Samuel was uneasy about this request, and when he consulted God, God said, "Listen to all that the people are saying to you; it is not you they have rejected, but they have rejected me as their king" (1 Samuel 8:7 ESV). In other words, God was telling Samuel that people want an earthly leader to follow so that they don't have to follow their spiritual leader. Instead of their heavenly King, they wanted an earthly king.

Before granting their request, Samuel first warned the Jews about desiring a king. He told them that a king would exploit them, would take their money and resources, would send their sons off to battle, and would make them his slaves, and "when that day comes, you will cry out for relief from the king you have chosen, but the Lord will not answer you in that day" (1 Samuel 8:18 ESV). Despite his warnings, in 1 Samuel 8:19–20 (ESV), it says, "But the people refused to listen to Samuel. 'No!' they said. 'We want a king over us. Then we will be like all the other nations, with a king to lead us and to go out before us and fight our battles.'"

I love that last line there in verse 20. The Jews wanted a king *to fight their battles for them*. When we look at politics today, are we really that different? It is human nature to desire to be led. That is why we have our Father, our King in heaven, to lead and to shepherd us. Yet when we forget this, we turn to the leaders of this world as a cheap substitute and run the risk of making the leaders of earth our idols.

Instead of putting in the work ourselves, it is so tempting to elect leaders who will fight our literal and metaphorical battles for us. We love to delegate the difficult task of enacting God's kingdom here on earth to a handful of people so that we no longer have to think about it. It is much easier to vote than to actually take care of the poor, the oppressed, and the marginalized. It is simpler to blame someone else for our own shortcomings as believers than to take responsibility for our own inaction.

For example, I know hundreds of Christians who claim to be super "passionate" about abortion and gay marriage, and yet I know very few Christians who have actually done something to provide mothers with an alternative to aborting their baby (e.g., monetary or emotional support, adoption opportunities, volunteering with low-income, at-risk females, mentoring youth before they make that decision, etc.) or have actually spent time with someone in the LGBTQIA community to share the gospel and Christ's love with them. Similarly, I know many Christians who are super "passionate" about economic and racial inequality, but outside of posting a few things on social media, their social, professional, and financial habits do not reflect a genuine desire to lay down their own rights and privilege to put the needs of others first. *It is not the Republican or Democratic Party's job to enact the work of Christ. It is our job to do that.*

As Christians, if we truly are that passionate about these issues, then instead of just talking the talk, we should be out there walking the walk, championing these causes, and making real impacts on our communities. However, it has become so easy to become apathetic in our faith and hide behind a ballot box and count it as our good deeds of the year, and some people don't even do that! In fact, for most people, they only seem to care about these issues in an election year when it is trendy and popular to be perceived as an activist. Once the election is over, most people go back to their daily lives, forgetting that these issues exist, hoping that politicians will just take care of these issues for them. Four years later, when things haven't changed, they get fired up again, pointing the finger at politics when, in reality, they haven't put any work in themselves.

Satan is probably sitting back and loving this. He would want nothing more than for us to focus all our time and energy on being petty in this world rather than doing the real work of God's kingdom. He wants us to talk a big talk without walking the walk. He wants us to be more concerned about being right than being righteous. He wants us to waste our time in service of an earthly king instead of our heavenly King. He thrives off of disunity, chaos, and fear.

There is something wrong with the Christian community if we are more willing to be vocal about our political beliefs than our religious beliefs. It's no wonder the US has a skewed idea of what being a Christian means. The political battle cries of the Christian electorate completely distract from what the true message of Christianity is all about. We are a large population with a loud voice, and unfortunately, I believe we are not using it where it counts. Our identity should be rooted in our heavenly citizenship, not our earthly citizenship. Our primary message should be about the good news of Christ, not a party platform or policy that is of this world and is destined to fail.

MAKING AN IDOL OUT OF OUR POLITICS

In 2018, well-known pastor Tim Keller wrote an article for the *New York Times* titled, "How Do Christians Fit into the Two-Party System? They Don't." Keller wrote that the problem with reconciling our religious beliefs and our political beliefs is that "historical Christian positions on social issues do not fit into contemporary political alignments."[45] Moreover, the issues that God cares about do not fit perfectly into the agendas of political parties. Therefore, how do we as Christians decide which issues are the most important? In other words, what political issues does God care about the most?

Stop right there. This is the problem with American Christians. We are so quick to pick out the issues that we think God cares about the "most." Republicans might say that God cares most about unborn babies and protecting the holy institution of marriage; Democrats might say that God cares most about socioeconomic and racial inequality. However, the reality is God cares about all issues equally in the sense that *He demands perfection in everything*. Nowhere in scripture does God say that you should just try to be "good enough." We are not just aiming for a passing grade. There is not a satisficing model of righteousness. God obviously cares about unborn babies, *and* people who are repressed, *and* the poor and marginalized, *and* human rights violations, *and* the freedom of God's people, *and* the justice system, *and* crime, *and* our health and well-being, *and* the exploitation of labor, *and* socioeconomic inequality, *and* war and peace. The list goes on and on. However, why do we let political parties set the agenda for us and tell us what issues are most important?

Ultimately, political parties are not conducive to achieving God's standards. They have to set an agenda and limit their priorities. In order to get elected, they have to make promises to many different groups of people, and Christians are just one of those groups. They are often beholden

---

[45] Timothy Keller, "How Do Christians Fit Into the Two-Party System? They Don't," *New York Times*, September 29, 2018, https://www.nytimes.com/2018/09/29/opinion/sunday/christians-politics-belief.html

to their donors and key stakeholders. They may have their own hidden agendas for power and prestige. They may have to neglect issues that they care about because they have limited time and resources. It is a politician's job to compromise, but God doesn't make compromises.

The reality is, when it comes to politics, Christians cannot win. We are voting for imperfect humans who are incapable of upholding God's standards for the world. When we vote, we know right off the bat that the person we are voting for is going to sin. In addition, we know that they are going to have to prioritize some issues over others. They might spend time and money on an issue that God cares about, but it might also be at the expense of another issue God cares about. Therefore, any time we are putting our confidence in the flesh, we will be disappointed.

Rom. 13 ?

So, why do we continue to put our confidence in the flesh? <u>God never desired for us to have earthly political leaders</u>. He wanted us to think that He was enough and that His kingdom was enough. Nevertheless, He let us indulge in our own stubbornness and pride because He gave us free will. We demanded a king, and so He gave us one. He warned us against putting our hopes in the powers of this world, but we did not listen. We have been so quick to make politics and our political leaders our idols.

However, God's redemption plan for creation was not and is not political. Jesus did not come down to earth to run for office and hopefully enact a handful of policies that give people a false sense of security and a belief that the world isn't that bad. Jesus's teachings were not a party platform or a blueprint for government. Jesus's goal wasn't just to make the world a better place or to just leave the world somewhat better off than He found it. He came to rescue us out of this world, because no matter how hard we try, our efforts to save the world are not enough. Therefore, we need to stop patting ourselves on the back for settling for a mirage of the kingdom of heaven instead of the real thing.

Furthermore, think about the disciples and early Christians. They were not concerned with how to reform the political institutions of the Roman Empire. Their time was not spent championing political policies or campaigning for political leaders. They were more concerned about sharing the good news of Christ. Their sights were set on eternity, and as a result, they did not get distracted from their ultimate mission.

I believe without a shadow of a doubt that if Jesus were here on earth, He would not identify with a political party but instead would identify with His heavenly Father. While we would be busy arguing about who we should vote for, Jesus would be out in the world making a real-life impact on the souls of His children. He would ask us, "Why are you so concerned about who should lead you here on earth when you can rest in the assurance that your heavenly Father has got it taken care of?" You only have a limited number of hours in your day. Would you rather use your time in service of a temporary political platform or leader or in service of Christ? Matthew 6:24 tells us that "no one can serve two masters. Either you will hate the one and love the other, or you will be devoted to the one and despise the other." Be honest with yourself. Who really is your master?

In 2020, during the #BlackLivesMatter protests, Christian hip-hop artist, KB, posted the following on social media: "How do I know if I have made an idol out of my politics? When you see the war on racism as a battle of the left vs the right INSTEAD of the kingdom of God vs the kingdom of darkness" (@kb_hga, June 2, 2020). This gave me chills because it perfectly articulated what I have been trying to explain for many years now. The left-right political cleavage runs so deep in our society that people are hardwired to think in that dichotomy. People have become so indoctrinated by their political party that they assume that every position that comes out of their political party is the gold standard of truth. They are so loyal to their political party that they are afraid to criticize their own political party and leaders even when their actions and beliefs are completely misaligned with scripture.

However, when we are talking about issues like racism, poverty, injustice, sexual assault, exploitation, life, and death, you are either on God's side or the side of the enemy. There is no in-between, and if you find yourself dancing around issues, justifying the actions of your political party, saying things like, "Well … it's complicated. What people on the left (or right) don't understand is …" frankly, you are a coward, and you have made an idol out of your politics. Injustice is not complicated. Things are either right or wrong. They are either from the Lord or from the enemy. Why is it that Christian Republicans are unwilling to speak out against racial injustice and Christian Democrats are unwilling to speak out against abortion? People are so afraid to not fit in with their political tribes that they cowardly stay silent on issues that God cares about, and somehow think that standing up on some issues, but not others, makes them morally justified.

We have become slaves to our political parties, willing to defend them at all costs even when we know their actions are sinful. We get so bogged down by the minutiae of an issue that we forget to first communicate God's heart on that issue. We are so willing to retweet what a politician or the media has said that we fail to even consider what God says. We are so lazy in our critical thinking that we are willing to take what the world says at face value without even considering whether it lines up with biblical truth or not. We do not take the time to ask ourselves how we are representing Christ when it comes to our politics.

Now I get it. I am a political scientist, and I would be the first to say that politics can be extremely complicated. We often don't know what the right policy solution is for extremely difficult issues. We might all agree that something is inherently good or bad but might disagree on what is the best path to get there. Politics is about winners and losers, and oftentimes there is no perfect *earthly* solution to meet the needs of everyone.

That being said, as Christians, we should first and foremost be united in our commitment to Christ. We should be the first to reach across party lines, to pool together our resources, knowing that the best solutions to the issues of this world come from Christ. There are some things that we might still disagree on, but they should be secondary to what we do all agree on, and that is that the world is broken and we are all in desperate need of a savior. In addition, if we truly believe as Christians that the world needs a spiritual solution, not just an earthly one, then our mindsets have to shift. Instead of fighting with the weapons of this world, we should be fighting with our spiritual weapons. When animosity between Democrats and Republicans increases, Christians should be the ones taking a step back to say we serve a God that is bigger than these left-right divisions. We will not succumb to the petty fights of this world because we need to save our energy for an even larger battle that is being fought.

Imagine what the US would be like if Christians really took this call seriously. Christians still make up a majority of the United States, and what if politicians truly had to cater to the Christian electorate to secure their votes, instead of just saying a few half-hearted platitudes to a lazy and ignorant target demographic? What is more, if Christians were truly championing the causes of Christ in their everyday lives, we would not feel the need to have politicians fill in the gaps. *Politics should not be a substitute for real kingdom work.*

Fellow Christians, we need to wake up! In a world that is promised to persecute us, we need to be alert and diligently seeking truth and not becoming tempted by other alternatives. Matthew 10:16 says, "I am sending you out like sheep among wolves. Therefore, be shrewd as snakes and innocent as doves." We should not allow ourselves to be manipulated. We should not allow ourselves to be taken advantage of. We should never blindly give our support to anyone or anything in this world. We need to be diligent, thoughtful, and prepared. We should research things for ourselves. We should not vote for someone just because someone else told us to or because everyone else is doing it. We need to utilize discernment.

I hate election times because it brings out the worst in the Christian community. I hear statements like "You can't be a Christian if you vote for this person or that person." I see Christians posting scathing political remarks on social media. I see Christians who are normally passive in their faith suddenly come out as "super religious," sending hypocritical and inconsistent messages to people who aren't believers. Think about the friends or community around you. If the only time they hear about your faith is when the topic of politics comes up, there is something wrong with that picture. It falsely communicates that God only matters when it comes to our politics.

In addition, think about how you utilize your social media platforms. I know many Christians who are quick to identify themselves on social media as a Republican or a Democrat, at the expense of identifying themselves as a citizen of heaven. Furthermore, we are so easily consumed by the echo chambers of our own political parties and are so susceptible to party propaganda that we no longer see the world through a biblical worldview but through a Republican or Democratic worldview. As a result, from an outsider's perspective, it would seem like our primary allegiance is to our political party, not to Christ. Our social media accounts look no different from our nonbeliever peers as we falsely communicate that we too have put our hope in this world, rather than in Christ.

As Christians, <u>we should be</u> preaching a message of reconciliation and of peace, and election times should radically amplify the beauty of Christian community. In addition, <u>we should be</u> reminding people that our hope is not in the things of this world and that earthly solutions are not enough to fix eternal problems. <u>My challenge to you</u> is instead of complaining about politics or pointing the finger at who you assume to be the problem, *go out and be the solution*. We are the hands and feet of Christ, and news stories should instead be focused on all the amazing work Christians and the church are doing in this country and around the world, as opposed to how we are tearing one another apart. The messages proclaimed by Christians <u>should</u> look different from the messages proclaimed by the Republican and Democratic parties. Our goals are not the same.

At the end of the day, I truly believe that God does not necessarily care about who we vote for. He cares about our hearts and whether we have a desire to glorify Him through our words and actions before, during, and after an election. Do we spend time in prayer, asking God for wisdom and discernment? Do we demonstrate compassion for the people who will be most affected by the election? Do we stand up for justice and biblical truth? Do we watch our tongues and exercise self-control? Are we motivated by selfishness, or do we desire to put others first? Are we proclaiming a message of peace and reconciliation, or are we stirring up unnecessary divisions? Are we serving as representatives for Christ or just representatives of an earthly institution? Do we put our hope in earthly solutions to earthly problems, or are we looking toward Jesus as our savior and redeemer? These are the things God cares about.

This is not to say that there aren't some candidates who are better suited for a position of power than others. I am also not trying to say that we cannot still be wise about our vote choice or to be engaged in politics. When it comes to election times, I believe that the best thing you can do as a Christian is to seriously pray about your vote, do some research, seek wise counsel from other mature believers, consult scripture, ask God for guidance, and use your convictions to make your decision. If you have done these things, then it is not my job as a fellow believer to tell you to go against your convictions. That is why we have been given the Holy Spirit, to enable us to access the wisdom and direction of Christ. Furthermore, as believers <u>we should not</u> stay silent on issues of injustice and therefore, at times, will need to stand up in the political realm for things that we believe in. It would be tempting to become complacent, under the guise of "not wanting to get involved in politics," but not speaking up and standing up for truth is also a sin. That means we may even have to speak out against areas of injustice perpetrated by members of our own political party.

I also truly believe that politics can be an incredibly useful tool for believers. Politics opens up opportunities for conversation that can be utilized to point people to Jesus and the kingdom of heaven. Unfortunately, I also think that, as believers, we are wasting these opportunities and are forgetting that the gospel is our primary message. People are craving to have conversations about the things that matter in this life, and the topic of politics can be utilized as a vessel for more meaningful dialogue. We should be ready as believers to enter into this dialogue to offer hope and to point people to our collective need of a savior.

At the end of the day, the true purpose of this chapter is not to say that we can't be engaged in politics, but to warn believers about falling into the trap of putting our hope in anything other than Jesus Christ. Neither the Republican Party nor the Democratic Party is our savior, and our identity is not rooted in being an American; it is rooted in being a citizen of heaven. Therefore, who are we putting our hope in? Are we putting more faith into the words of politicians or in the Word of our Savior? Are we sitting back and hoping that our government will do God's work for us, or are we out in our communities preaching the gospel, standing up for biblical truth and justice, and loving people like Christ?

CHAPTER 8
CHECK YOUR PRIVILEGE

Gone are the days I'm chasing after what won't last
I'm done with building these castles that crumble like sand
Oh, knees on the floor
I finally found that everything I needed was always right in front of me
You gave me a name
You changed everything

—"Till I Found You" by Phil Wickham

I will be the first to admit that I am a basic white girl. I love fall and all things pumpkin spice; I frequently scroll through Instagram and Pinterest; I wear leggings mostdays; I go to Target and Trader Joes on a weekly basis and almost always buy something that I don't need; I love eating healthy but also never turn down Chick-fil-A; I watch shows like *The Bachelor*, *Gossip Girl*, *The O.C.*, *Pretty Little Liars*, *Gilmore Girls*, and *Riverdale*; and I am addicted to iced coffee and sparkling water.

I will also be the first to admit though that I have had the privileges of a basic white girl as well. I grew up in classic suburbia in a great school district. I was upper-middle class and got to do things like go on vacation and go out to eat. I lived in a safe neighborhood in a gated community on a man-made lake and never had to share a room. My parents were both educators, and so I was always raised with the expectation that I would go to college and that I could be whatever I wanted to be. We went to an awesome church where I got to be a part of a super fun youth group and have mentors who were not my parents. I had lots of friends and was well liked in school, so I always felt a sense of belonging and significance. I got to take ballet and piano lessons, play both school and club volleyball, have birthday parties, and hang out with my friends. I had a part-time job in high school working as a nanny and as a barista, but it was so I could have extra spending money in college.

Even writing this now, I am sick to my stomach thinking about how privileged I am and how my normal is so incredibly rare in the world we live in today. Therefore, I do not say these things to subtly brag about how "fortunate" I am (#blessed) but to openly acknowledge the ways in which my privilege as an upper-middle class, educated, white American has advantaged me in this life and how my perceptions of what is "normal" have been completely distorted by my own life experiences.

I totally understand that many of my readers might not be coming from the same place of privilege as myself. Many of you have probably faced extreme hardships, such as poverty or financial instability, racial discrimination, unstable family environments, physical or mental disabilities, illness, social isolation, and more and have had to overcome numerous hurdles over the course of your lifetime. Therefore, I do not want to come across as insensitive or ignorant, or presume that my normal is the default.

However, I am writing this chapter because I also understand that many of my readers are coming from similar places of privilege and need a wake-up call in regard to how that privilege has become a major stumbling block in advancing the kingdom of heaven, particularly in the United States. In many ways, evangelical Christianity in the United States has become conflated with middle-class, suburban, white America in ways that are incredibly dysfunctional for the faith at large, and although no one really wants to talk about it, someone needs to call it like it is. I think it is important for me to role model what it looks like to "check your privilege" and to acknowledge the ways in which our privilege is keeping us from becoming more like Christ.

To begin, the Bible is very clear that everything of this world is rubbish when compared to the surpassing worth of Christ, and that we should be willing to lose everything in this world for the sake of knowing Christ

(Philippians 3:8). When Jesus tells His disciples to pick up their cross and follow Him, He asks them to give up everything and reminds them in Matthew 16:26, "What good will it be for someone to gain the whole world, yet forfeit their soul?"

And yet we are so prone to pride that we falsely attribute the blessings in our lives to our own hard work and merit and are unwilling to walk away from our privilege, because we think that we deserve it. In doing so, we also forget to praise God for the blessings in our lives, failing to recognize that at the end of the day, we are nothing without Christ and what we really deserve is death.

In Deuteronomy 8:10–14, it says, "When you have eaten and are satisfied, praise the Lord your God for the good land he has given you. Be careful that you do not forget the Lord your God, failing to observe his commands, his laws and his decrees that I am giving you this day. Otherwise, *when you eat and are satisfied, when you build fine houses and settle down, and when your herds and flocks grow large and your silver and gold increase and all you have is multiplied, then your heart will become proud and you will forget the Lord your God.*" (emphasis added) ??

Although these verses were written in the seventh century BC, I am struck by how applicable they are today. It is easy to imagine a twenty-first-century version of this passage that paints a picture of the American dream, with Christians settling in comfortably to their safe little bubbles, patting themselves on the back for all that they have accomplished. Basically, what Moses is saying here in the book of Deuteronomy is that over time, the more we accumulate, the more successes we have, the more we increase in our status ... the more we also increase in our pride.

We begin to think that everything we have was earned by our own merit. When we get that college degree, we think, *Man, I worked hard for this; this was well deserved,* rather than praising the Lord for giving us the opportunity to go to school in the first place. When we buy our first house, we think of what a smart financial investment we are making and how proud we are of how much we saved up, rather than thanking the Lord for providing us with a job, financial security, and access to resources that helped us make this financial decision. When we finish that marathon, we think of how much we trained for this moment, rather than appreciating the fact that God gave us an able body and the luxury of free time to be able to train and run for fun.

First Corinthians 4:7 (NASB) also states, "For who regards you as superior? What do you have that you did not receive? And if you did receive it, why do you boast as if you had not received it?" Nothing we have is earned or deserved. Everything that we have is a gift from God, even life itself, so why do we strut about as if we are someone worthy of praise? This verse is basically God calling us out asking, "Who in the world do you think you are?"

Therefore, step one in checking our privilege is to recognize who we are in relation to Christ. It requires an attitude of humility and thankfulness. Instead of boasting about our accomplishments, status, and strengths, we should instead be "boasting in our weaknesses" so that the power of Christ can work through us (2 Corinthians 12:9). Our weaknesses are the only things we can give up to God that He doesn't already have, meaning we should be more focused on how we can utilize our hardships and shortcomings to magnify God's greatness, not our own. In contrast, the blessings in our life should be a reminder of our own unworthiness and, as a result, should give us a greater appreciation of the grace that has been given to us.

Step two, however, is to also recognize that we live in a broken world that has arbitrarily bestowed more privilege on some people than others. Whether it is because of the color of your skin, or your gender, or your family background, or the country you grew up in, or your socioeconomic status, or the talents you were born with, some people have inherited more privilege than others.

Ever since the Fall, society has embarked on a downward trajectory of sin and brokenness that has created a world that is messed up. We have created systems of oppression that have advantaged some over others. We have exploited individuals and societies for economic and political gain. We have neglected the needs of the poor and the marginalized. We have passively sat by while injustices have occurred. And we have justified all of it on the false basis of merit and deservingness. With false doctrines such as *survival of the fittest* or *what comes around goes around*, we somehow believe that we have earned the right to sit on our thrones of privilege. As a result, we continue to perpetuate systems of violence against people who have been made in the image of God, because we have become comfortable in our pride.

This is why we are all, both individually and collectively as a society, in need of a savior. Left to our own devices, it is our nature to mess everything up. We have taken the beautiful picture of God's creation and ripped it to pieces. As a result, the world today looks nothing like what God had originally intended. God did not create human beings in His own image so that we can put others down and spend a lifetime competing with one another, trying to decide who is the "best," and arguing over who "deserves" what. Who are we to say that one image of God is better than another? Why are we so quick to think that God likes us, or people like us, best? Why are we so quick to justify our actions because they are at least "better" than the person next to us?

No matter where you come from or what your background is, we have all been influenced by the type of worldly thinking that is obsessed with the hierarchy and where our place is within it. The world judges based on what we have. People are valued based on the level of wealth, status, race, success, gender, accomplishments, possessions, and accolades they have. A person's worth in the world is thus defined by where they reside in the hierarchy, and people begin to believe that they deserve to be where they are at, or that they deserve to be at the top even when they are not. Everyone wants to move up the hierarchy. No one wants to be at the bottom. However, this is dangerous thinking. The more we obsess over the hierarchy, the more we forget that Jesus came to abolish the hierarchy, to turn the hierarchy on its head, where the last becomes first and the first becomes last.

The world honestly needs a serious reboot. We aren't even able to comprehend how far we have strayed from God's original plan, and the reality is we are only going to continue to make things worse. Until Jesus comes back though, we aren't just supposed to passively sit back and think to ourselves, *Life is unfair, but people need to just get over it. Things are the way they are.*

Not only does God remind us that everything we have is not our own and that we need to be vigilant about checking our privilege so that we don't become proud, but also God goes one step further in Luke 12:48, which states, "From everyone who has been given much, much will be demanded; and from the one who has been entrusted with much, much more will be asked." The blessings we have been given or have inherited are not for our gratification but to bring glory to God and to be utilized for His divine purposes.

Luke 12:48 is the verse that keeps me up at night.

If my calculations are correct, I have a lot to live up to because I have been given a lot. The more privilege I have, the more I am called to do something with that privilege. In addition, I now have to actively fight even harder against all that is keeping me distracted from what is truly important in life. It is easy to be comfortable, but we aren't called to be comfortable. It is easy to be complacent, but we aren't called to be complacent. At the end of my life, I am going to have to answer to the almighty God and attest to how I utilized the blessings He entrusted me with to bless others and His kingdom. And what if I had just sat back, comfortable and complacent, forgetting to acknowledge the blessings God has given me and failing to ask God how I might use those blessings for His kingdom, and then obey? That image terrifies me.

Now I first need to clarify that the Bible is also very clear that our salvation is not based on works. Ephesians 2:8–10 says, "For it is by grace you have been saved, through faith—and this is not from yourselves, it is the gift of God—not by works, so that no one can boast. For we are God's handiwork, created in Christ Jesus to do good works, which God prepared in advance for us to do." Therefore, we will fall short. We will fail to act. We will become entitled and comfortable and complacent. But thank goodness there is grace and that our salvation is not dependent on our actions.

However, there is a reason why the Bible says it is easier for a camel to go through the eye of a needle than a rich man to get into the kingdom of heaven (Matthew 19:24). Whereas the world sees money, success, and accomplishments as a good thing, the Bible says that these things are only inhibitors keeping us from Christ. What the world views as privilege, God views as a stumbling block. When the world has been kind to us and has elevated our status, we are tempted to put our hope in the world. We become blinded by the false promises that the world has to offer, and we lose sight of Christ and our need for a savior.

DON'T JUST CHECK YOUR PRIVILEGE.
DO SOMETHING WITH IT.

White privilege. Male privilege. Socioeconomic privilege. American privilege. Able-bodied privilege. Privilege that comes from being attractive, popular, or famous. Privilege in possessions. Privilege in talent or giftings. Privilege in knowledge and resources. What if, as Christians, we were driven by a desire to identify, check, and utilize our privilege to bring glory to God and to proclaim His message throughout the world? What if instead of attacking people's privilege or defending our own privilege, we all just had an attitude that said, *Here I am, here is what the Lord has given me, and what can I do with it to glorify Him?*

What if we as Christians had an aversion to privilege? What if we all took active steps to remove ourselves from our privilege? What if we took the Bible seriously when it says in 1 John 2:15, "Do not love the world or anything in the world. If anyone loves the world, the love of the Father is not in him. For all that is in the world—the desires of the flesh, the desires of the eyes, and the pride of life—is not from the Father but from the world. The world and its desires pass away, but whoever does the will of God lives forever"? The world would be a different place. Instead of racing to the top of the hierarchy, we would all be shedding our privilege in its many forms.

In doing so, the goal is not to then boast about our own magnanimity or to feel a sense of superiority for how self-sacrificing we have become. It would be easy to get caught up in the white savior complex, calling attention to how "woke" we are in order to receive the accolades of our peers. Instead, we should, as Philippians 2:3–4 tells us, "Do nothing out of selfish ambition or vain conceit. Rather, in humility value others above yourselves, not looking to your own interests but each of you to the interests of the others."

Therefore, we could all use a reality check. We need to take the time to examine our hearts before the Lord and be honest with ourselves about stumbling blocks in our lives that are preventing us from having an attitude of humility and compassion. Below are some questions I encourage you to ask yourself:

"Go. Sell all that you have and give it to the poor."

❑ Am I quick to believe that I "deserve" the things in my life or that I have "earned" them by my own merit?

❑ Am I quick to cast judgment on others who are "less fortunate" than I am and attribute their life circumstances to their inferior decision-making?

❑ Do I forget to practice humility in both my thoughts and actions?

❑ Am I falling short when it comes to using my blessings to bless others around me?

❑ Do I perpetuate systems of this world rather than advocating for what God's original design was for creation?

❑ Am I prone to justify things for being the way that they are, rather than acknowledging the way that things fall short from God's standards?

❑ Am I uncomfortable acknowledging my own blessings and privilege?

❑ Is it easy for me to become complacent in regard to injustice in the world?

❑ Do I feel pride over where I am at in the world's hierarchy?

❑ Am I satisfied with the status quo?

❑ Do I feel threatened when people call out the areas of privilege in my life?

❑ Am I more prone to be defensive of my thoughts and actions, rather than acknowledging the ways that I have perhaps been ignorant or insensitive?

❑ Do I see myself as being superior to others around me?

❑ Could I be more generous with my time, energy, and/or resources?

❑ Do I see the church as an institution that should provide services for me, rather than asking how I can be in service of the church in order to meet the needs of others?

❑ Do I shy away from opportunities where I can stand up for the oppressed?

❑ Do I value my own safety and security over the safety and security of others?

❑ Are my hopes set on the American dream rather than Christ's plan for my life?

If your answer was yes to any of these questions (which <u>should be</u> all of you if you are being honest with yourself), then I encourage you to do some serious heart work, asking God to reveal to you the areas in your life that could use an attitude makeover.

Privilege has become somewhat of a buzzword in society, which has its pros and cons. Although talking about privilege more does increase people's knowledge and awareness on the issue, at the same time, people are skeptical of buzzwords, assuming they are indicative of some political agenda. However, we cannot as Christians ignore biblical concepts just because they have been given a new name. Yes, terms like "white privilege" and "male privilege" are not found in scripture, but the concepts of humility, empathy, compassion, and laying down our rights for the sake of others are at the core of the gospel.

When we look to the life of Jesus, we see a perfect example of someone who denied Himself all His rights and shed any form of privilege He had to lay down His life for us. As the Son of the almighty God, Jesus could have easily rested in the comfort and glory of His position. Instead, He humbled himself, taking on the form of a man, to be beaten, despised, mocked, and even killed for the sake of the "least of these." He was not concerned with what He deserved as God's Son, nor was He quick to discredit others because of their "unworthiness." He did not see people through hierarchical lenses created by humankind but instead elevated the status of the poor, the oppressed, the voiceless, the destitute, the widows, and the orphans.

He also consistently called out people with positions of power, pointing to their pride, greed, self-indulgence, and abuse of their power. In Jewish culture, <u>no one had more privilege than the Pharisees</u>, who were deemed superior for their education, gender, wealth, political status, <u>ethnicity,</u> and family bloodlines. However, Jesus criticized the Pharisees more than anyone else in scripture. In Matthew 23, Jesus literally says seven times, "You Pharisees and teachers of the Law of Moses are in for trouble! You're nothing but show-offs." Jesus then tells them in verses 11–12, "The greatest among you will be your servant. For those who exalt themselves will be humbled, and those who humble themselves will be exalted."

In other words, when your status has been elevated by society, bestowing upon you an earthly form of "greatness," your immediate reaction should be to humble yourself and to utilize your position to serve others. I wish we viewed privilege like a game of hot potato, where everyone is trying to get rid of their privilege as fast as they can. This is unfortunately not the world we live in. However, we can all strive to examine the areas of our life that can be better utilized to serve others in society who have not been given the same privileges as us.

I have been given a great education. I can use that to educate others and to open people's eyes to injustice. I am considered wealthy by the standards of the world. I can use my money to help those in need. I live in a democracy where I have the right to follow Jesus. I can use my freedom to bring freedom to others. I am white. I can use my historical position of power to champion the causes of the oppressed. I am able-bodied. I can be the hands and feet of Jesus. I have a loving and supportive family. I can go out of my way to make people feel included and cherished. I have a house. I can use it to practice hospitality to those around me. I have a voice. I can use that voice to speak God's truth and call out injustice. I have a platform. I can use that platform to proclaim the good news of Christ.

When we stand before the almighty God, we will be judged not by worldly standards of success but rather by our humility and our willingness to lay our lives down for the sake of Christ. We should not confuse the American dream as our spiritual calling from Christ. Living in an upper-middle class household in suburbia with an excellent school district, two to three kids, stable jobs and incomes, a great 401(k), and a vacation home are not necessarily bad things in and of themselves, but they are not the end goal, and we cannot allow ourselves to make these things our idols. Furthermore, we cannot treat these things as signals of some demented form of righteousness that allows us to feel morally superior to those who have not "achieved" the same "blessings" in their lives. I would rather be poor and oppressed and on fire for Jesus than safe and secure and apathetic in my faith.

This is why we could all use a wake-up call as believers. The world's rubric for success is diametrically opposed to God's rubric of righteousness, and the desires of the flesh are in competition with our desire for holiness. We do not want to go on falsely thinking that we are winning at life, only to show up at the pearly gates and have God tell us that He never knew us (Matthew 7:21–23). The most joyful and hope-filled people in the Bible are not the ones who "had it all together" but the ones who fully realized that everything is rubbish when compared to the surpassing greatness of knowing Christ.

Therefore, as believers, may we all be known for giving away more than we receive. May we be known for our humility, not our pride. May we be constantly elevating others above ourselves, rather than striving for what we think we deserve. May we see every blessing as an opportunity to bless others. May we not confuse the American dream with our spiritual calling from Christ. May we find our identities in Christ, rather than our worldly accomplishments or status. May we all hold one another accountable for checking our privilege and doing something with it. May we all ask for forgiveness when we fall short.

At the end of the day, the only hierarchy we should perpetuate is the one that puts Christ and others ahead of us.

CHAPTER 9
GOD IS NOT WHITE. OR AMERICAN.

I can see Your heart
Eight billion different ways
Every precious one
A child You died to save
If You gave Your life to love them so will I

—"So Will I (100 Billion X)" by Hillsong Worship

I *love* to travel and have actually been to twenty-five different countries over the course of my lifetime. Although twenty-five definitely sounds a lot, it is nothing compared to the number of countries each of my parents have gone to. Between my mom's backpacking through Europe days in college, my dad's stint as a semiprofessional basketball player, the year my parents spent in the Caribbean teaching at an international school, and their more recent obsession with cruises, my parents are the most well-traveled people I know.

Because of my jet-setter parents, at a very young age, I was exposed to how big the world truly is. The summer in between third and fourth grade was the first time we traveled as a family internationally. Our really good family friends felt called to plant a church in Amsterdam, so we went to go visit them, hitting up the UK, France, and Belgium while we were out there. The following summer, my parents (who are educators) volunteered to chaperone a student exchange program that sent high school students to Japan every year, and they got to bring my brother and me along with them.

Therefore, by the time I was eleven, I was already among some of the most well-traveled people in America. To say that I had caught the travel bug would be an understatement. I was (and still am) obsessed with international travel. I have toured businesses in India with my MBA program, practiced my Spanish on a summer-long missions trip to El Salvador, road Vespas through the Tuscan countryside with my husband, visited the homeland of my ancestors with my family in Scotland, laid on a beach sipping cocktails in Thailand, visited the tallest building in the world (at the time) in China, built houses in Mexico with high schoolers, and nerded out over *Star Wars* filming spots in Croatia, yet every time I travel to a new place, I am just struck by how big the world is and how small and insignificant my life is compared to all God's creation around the world.

Unfortunately, not everyone has had the privilege to be able to travel the world, and I know that I am incredibly fortunate to have gotten to experience so much of what the world has to offer. I wish though that everyone had the opportunity to travel internationally because you are able to see, in a very tangible way, how diverse God's creation truly is. My international travels have opened my eyes to different people, different customs, different languages, different cultures, different needs, and different perspectives.

I remember sitting on an air-conditioned bus traveling through a shanty town neighborhood in India and thinking to myself, *Wow, I am literally on the opposite side of the globe right now, so far away from my safe little community bubble, and yet God is here in this shanty town in India, just like He is in my little suburb back home.* I had traveled 8,290 miles but was the same distance away from God.

I became so overwhelmed by the fact that my life experiences and perspective on God represented just an infinitesimal fraction of the ways God connected with His people across time and space. It was like being a puzzle piece in a thousand-piece puzzle that just discovered that their small corner of the puzzle and the few puzzle pieces around it were only a fraction of the entire puzzle. All this time, the puzzle piece thought the puzzle was a picture of a just a tree, when instead the tree was just one tree in an entire forest, that was situated near a lake, that was on top of hill, that was full of colorful flowers, that were all beneath a beautiful sky that was speckled with clouds! All this time, the puzzle piece thought that greens and browns were the best colors, because that was what it was used to, but when it saw the entire puzzle put together, it realized that the puzzle would not be the same if there weren't also blues, and pinks, and yellows, and oranges, and grays, and purples.

Now multiply that thousand-piece puzzle by a few million, and that is more like the puzzle we are dealing with today. There are now almost eight billion people in the world, and I am just one of them. There are almost 200 countries in the world, and I have lived in just one of them. There are several thousand spoken languages in the world, and I just speak one of them (unless you count my mediocre, high school–level, Spanish-speaking skills). There are millions of churches in the world, and I have gone to just a handful of them. There are thousands of Christian denominations ? in the world, and I have just practiced one of them (ironically called nondenominational). There are 2.18 billion Christians in the world, and I have interacted with barely a fraction of them.

Therefore, who am I to say that my personal experience with Christ is the right way or the only way to experience Christ? That would not only be incredibly close-minded and self-absorbed of me, but it would also be limiting the power of Christ to just one time, place, culture, and personal experience.

I want to first be clear here though that I am not trying to say that all paths lead to heaven. The Bible is pretty clear that Jesus is "the way, the truth, and the life," and that "no one comes to the father, except through [Jesus]" (John 14:6). In addition, Roman 10:9 says that you will be saved only if you "confess with your mouth that Jesus is Lord and believe in your heart that God has raised Him from the dead." Thus, I am not preaching a doctrine of cultural relativism in which knowledge, truth, and morality are not absolute and are subject to interpretation.

I am, however, trying to point out that a white, Americanized version of Christianity is not universal, not even by a long shot. Although the US still has the largest Christian population in the world, with 167 million,[46] the number of Christians across the globe is rapidly increasing, particularly in nonwhite, non-Western, non-English-speaking countries. Today there are now more Christians living in the global south than the global north.[47] The World Economic Forum estimates that by 2060, six out of the ten largest Christian populations will be in Africa.[48] China has seen a 10 percent increase in their Christian population each year since 1979, now totaling approximately fifty-four million, despite the efforts of the atheist Communist Party to squash that growth.[49] Even in Muslim majority nations, Christianity is on the rise, and Christianity is actually experiencing one of the fastest-growing church movements in Iran, even though most Christians still have to meet in secret.[50]

As a result, there is no such thing as the *average* Christian experience. Even if we picked a Christian at random in the world, there is only a 7.7 percent chance they would be an American. Moreover, it would be far more likely that the average Christian would be a nonwhite, non-American individual most likely living in poverty.

Therefore, our God did not send His Son to earth to die on a cross so that upper-middle class white people in America could sit safely in their pews singing a few half-hearted worship songs. Jesus came to save all people from all nations from all cultural backgrounds. The beauty in His message is that it is the same for a Silicon Valley tech worker, a coffee bean farmer in Costa Rica, a beach bum in Australia, a politician in South Korea, a maid working at a resort in the Bahamas, a French au pair, a

[46] Christopher Vondracek, "Number of Christians in U.S. has declined by 13 million since 2009, says Pew Research Center data," *The Washington Times,* October 17, 2019, https://www. washingtontimes.com/news/2019/oct/17/number-of-christians-in-us-has-declined-by-13-mill/
[47] Aaron Earls, "7 Surprising Trends in Global Christianity in 2019," *Facts & Trends,* June 11, 2019, https://factsandtrends.net/2019/06/11/7-surprising-trends-in-global-christianity-in-2019/
[48] Yomi Kazeen, "By 2060, six of the world's 10 largest Christian countries will be in Africa," *World Economic Forum,* April 10 2019, https://www.weforum.org/agenda/2019/04/africa-is-set-to-be-the-global-center-of-christianity-for-the-next-50-years/
[49] Eleanor Albert "Christianity in China," *Council on Foreign Relations,* October 11, 2018, https://www.cfr.org/backgrounder/christianity-china
[50] Stoyan Zaimov, "Iran Is Witnessing 'One of Fastest Growing Church Movements,' but Christians Face Intense Persecution," *Christian Post,* October 16, 2018, https://www.christianpost.com/news/iran-is-witnessing-one-of-fastest-growing-church-movements-but-christians-face-intense-persecution.html

religious cleric in Saudi Arabia, a Sherpa in Nepal, a teacher in Nigeria, a tribal chief from the Amazon, and a factory worker in Bangladesh.

In fact, many people in the Christian community believe that Jesus will not return until every nation and people group have heard the gospel. Matthew 24:14 says that the "gospel of the kingdom will be preached in the whole world as a testimony to *all nations*, and then the end will come." Later, in Revelation 7:9 (ESV), John describes his vision of end-times and says, "After this I looked, and behold, a great multitude that no one could number, *from every nation, from all tribes and peoples and languages*, standing before the throne and before the Lamb, clothed in white robes, with palm branches in their hands." (empasis added)

The good news of Jesus Christ was not intended for just one small homogenous group of people. This should inspire us to not only "go and make disciples of all nations" (Matthew 28: 19) but also to embrace the fact that there is beauty in a message that is intended to unify all nations, tribes, and tongues. Recognizing the vast diversity in human experience should only make us worship God even more. We serve a God who can connect with anyone, anywhere. There is no human experience too complicated for God to work through. There is no person or culture that is too difficult for God to reach.

I also want to emphasize that our God is a personal God who created all humankind in His own image and has a unique personal relationship with each one of His children. Currently, I have two babies under the age of two, and so I cannot really compare how my parenting style might change from one child to the next. However, I do remember being incredibly frustrated as a kid when my parents took one approach with me and another approach with my younger brother.

Now that I am older though, I realize how important it was for my parents to connect with my brother, who is a completely different kid, in a completely different way than they connected with me. What worked with me was never going to work with my brother. We had different personalities, different goals, different life experiences, different strengths, different weaknesses. It wasn't that one approach was better than the other or that my parents had different values or standards for parenting me versus my brother. They just knew that what worked with one kid wasn't going to work in the same way with their other kid.

In the same way, God chooses to connect with His children in ways that fit their natural and unique bent. He speaks to His children in different ways. He uses different life experiences to teach them different lessons. He uses different analogies to illustrate different messages. He can even use different pop culture references if He wants to drive home a particular point.

However, like most kids in the US, we like to think that we are the favorite child. In the words of Blake Shelton, we like to think that we live in "God's country." We like to believe that God connects with us more than all His kids, that our secret handshakes and inside jokes are His favorite. We are unable to fully comprehend how God can love each and every one of us equally. His interactions with His other children sometimes feel foreign to us (pun intended).

For example, the summer after my sophomore year in college, I went on a summer project with CRU to El Salvador. Summer projects were six weeklong missions trips centered around college campuses around the world where the gospel of Christ was shared with college students by college students. I had an amazing experience in El Salvador. I absolutely loved my team and the people of El Salvador and learned so much about God's character on that trip.

However, in the middle of our six-week missions trip, the universities we were working at took a short break from classes (I think because of a national holiday). Since there were no students on campus, our team went on a short retreat a few hours outside of San Salvador. The retreat was put on by some of the local Salvadorian students we were partnering with, and we were their guests for the weekend.

Although I was initially very excited about our little getaway, I quickly realized that I was not prepared for the cultural differences associated with the retreat portion of the trip. Salvadorans are incredibly friendly, kind, and hospitable, but their concept of time is completely different from ours here in America. Although there was a loose schedule prepared for the retreat, I don't think anyone looked at the schedule once. One afternoon, we went on a three-hour prayer hike that seemed to go on for forever. At night, the Salvadorans would take turns sharing what God had done in their lives around the campfire, but their stories would go on for hours. Right when you thought you were singing the last worship song for the session, a new set would begin. For me and my Type A personality, it was painful. I have never been so anxious to leave somewhere in my life. I have always been used to church activities having an end time and was not prepared for the spontaneity and lack of structure of the trip.

In retrospect, however, I not only needed to repent of my impatience, pride, and critical attitude, but I wish I would have enjoyed and appreciated the way that the Salvadorans connected with and worshipped God more. I was so out of my comfort zone that I was missing out on the beautiful authenticity exhibited by the Salvadorans. Whereas, in the United States, we often put God on a timeline and fit our time with God into neatly scheduled sessions, the way the Salvadorans experienced God was much more fluid and spontaneous. I was seeing a whole different side of my heavenly Father, and I was too distracted to notice and appreciate it.

As I look back on that experience, it is so clear to me that God connects with different people across different cultures in different ways. God can show up in a prayer walk that ends up taking hours longer than expected, but He can also show up in a scheduled morning quiet time before work. God is as alive and active in a church singing hymns as He is in a church with an upbeat gospel choir. God is not confined within one set of cultural values.

OUR SKEWED PERCEPTION OF THE CHURCH

We serve a big God. A global God. A multicultural, multiethnic, multicolored God. Therefore, our understanding of Christianity cannot be based on a skewed perception of the church arbitrarily defined by Western white America in the twenty-first century. It should be celebrated that our heavenly Father has made billions of unique individuals who are all in His image, who He has connected with personally across different cultures, civilizations, and time periods.

I think there are two different groups in particular that need to hear this. On the one hand, there are many Christians in America who have grown up in the typical white American church, and their only experience with church has been this particular format. They may have never experienced a church that was different from what they are used to and perhaps have never even considered that church could look different. As a result, it becomes easy for perceptions of Christianity to become

Not all Christians in America are white!

clouded by the familiar, the comfortable, the known. Furthermore, it is human nature to take what is known and what is familiar and ascribe to it a certain sense of superiority. This particular way of doing things must be right, because it is how I am used to doing it. As a result, we look down on people, customs, traditions, and practices that look different from our own because they represent "the other." We then feel a sense of "moral obligation" to "enlighten" these "backward people" who are "ignorant" to the "right" way of doing things.

This is the danger of experiencing only one type of church. If you have never experienced an alternative, how do you know which one is the best? Here I am not trying to argue that all churches are created equal. The Bible is pretty clear that we need to be wary of false teaching and false doctrines that are often perpetuated by the church. Indeed, there are many churches out there that are not interpreting scripture correctly (either unknowingly or even knowingly) and are leading God's children astray. That being said, we do need to be cognizant of our own cultural biases when evaluating what a church should or shouldn't look like. Who are we to limit the ability of God to connect with His children through various traditions and customs?

Although it would be easy to point the finger at this group of people who have only ever experienced one type of church and call them narrow-minded, sheltered, unsophisticated, or provincial, that assessment is not entirely fair. Most people around the world only have had one type of church experience that has dominated their outlook on the faith. Whether you are from a small African village, an American suburb, or a large Asian city, people are creatures of habit and stick with what they know. What is more, most people do not have the privilege or luxury of exploring different church options. There may only be one church available in their hometown. They may only be welcome at one type of church. For some, going to church may even be illegal, and meeting in secret in someone's house is the only option.

As a result, it is not realistic to prescribe to all Christians that they should travel the world (or even their country) to check out a variety of church formats before forming their opinion of the church. We can, though, learn to appreciate the fact that God works in ways that we don't fully understand and that our experience with God represents just a miniscule fraction of all the ways God has connected with His children. We can then look forward to the day in heaven when people from all tribes and tongues come together to worship God, finally enabling us to see the full puzzle with all its billions of pieces come together.

Now, on the other hand, there are also many people in America who criticize the church, along with Christianity, because they have also only experienced one version of church. The irony here is that they often criticize the church for being too white or too Western when they themselves have never ventured out to experience or explore the diversity in church experiences in the US or around the world. To say that the church is too white or too Western is to discount the church experiences of millions of people around the world. It presumes that the white American church is the default.

As a result, there are too many people who have written off Christianity because of their interactions with American Christians. However, have they even considered why there are millions of people across the globe who are literally willing to die for their faith, or why Christianity is booming in places that have actively tried to squash the efforts of Christians? I will be the first to admit that the American brand of Christianity has been losing favor over the past few decades and that we are not doing a good job representing Christ well here in America. However, it just kills me that, as a result, Christianity as a whole is being judged by the actions of middle-class white Americans who only represent a tiny fraction of Christians all around the world. When people say that Christians are hypocritical, close-minded, ultraconservative, entitled, ignorant, or sheltered, are they actually talking about Christians as a whole, or are they really just talking about a very specific American demographic?

Therefore, what if instead we all had a global perspective of Christianity? What if Christianity was no longer viewed through the lens of middle-class white America but was evaluated in its entirety? What if we truly believed that there was much to be learned from our brothers and sisters in Christ who have different cultural backgrounds, racial or ethnic identities, socioeconomic statuses, citizenship statuses, and international experiences? What if we saw each opportunity to interact with someone who is different from us as a unique opportunity to experience our heavenly Father in a new way? What if we saw God truly as a global God, rather than limiting

Him to one particular set of customs, traditions, and culture? What if we truly had the mindset that God loves every member of His family equally and that we are not the favorite child?

The world would honestly be a completely different place. Christianity would truly be a global movement, not just a local custom or norm. Christians would be challenged to get outside of their own little bubbles and would start to see the big global picture through God's eyes, not just the eyes of their local pastor or church. Maybe Christians who are free to practice their faith without persecution would no longer take that freedom for granted because they would recognize how many of their brothers and sisters in Christ are literally risking their lives and livelihoods to follow Christ. Maybe believers all around the world would feel emboldened because they would be more aware of all the ways God is moving in this world. Maybe Christians would be praised for the global unity that they foster rather than criticized for the divisions they create. And then, maybe we would see a revival here in America, because Christianity's brand would no longer be arbitrarily defined by Western white America.

CHAPTER 10
CAN A CHRISTIAN BE A FEMINIST?

I feel it in my bones, You're about to move
I feel it in the wind, You're about to ride in
You said that You would pour Your spirit out
You said that You would fall on sons and daughters
So like the rain, come and drench us in love
Let Your glory rush in like a flood
We are fixed on this one thing
To know Your goodness and see Your glory
We're transformed by this one thing
To know Your presence and see Your beauty

—"Spirit Move" by Bethel Music and Kalley Heiligenthal

It was a Wednesday afternoon, and I was sitting at a coffee shop by the beach with some friends of a friend whom I had just met. We were engaged in all kinds of interesting conversations when somehow the topic of feminism came up. The two guys I just met, one of them a pastor, were quick to scoff at the idea of feminism, immediately conjuring up images of a hippie lesbian who doesn't shave. I have never been one to keep my mouth shut when I disagree with someone, and so without pause I jumped in and said I consider myself to be a feminist. Their immediate response was that feminism was incompatible with Christianity. I disagreed and stated that I believe Jesus to be one of the first feminists and that it was not only possible but important to be a Christian feminist.

The discussion wasn't heated per se, but clearly none of us (including myself) were willing or open to having our opinions change. We were all more concerned with our interpretation of scripture being right than being concerned with whether Christ was being glorified through our actions and how the body of Christ could be doing better to proclaim the love of Christ in our communities. The conversation actually ended amicably, and they did concede that I knew my stuff and that I had raised some really good points; however, you could tell that at the end of the day, I hadn't changed their mind and that someday the topic of feminism would come up again, and we would all continue to make the same points and argue from the same perspective.

In retrospect though, I think one of the main issues that these guys couldn't get past was the actual word *feminism*. Even though I explained to them countless times that the definition of the word *feminism* was "the advocacy of women's rights on the basis of the equality of the sexes," in their minds, the word *feminism* was still mired with the liberal agenda, the pro-life/ pro-choice debate, and angry man-haters. It wasn't necessarily the case that they disagreed with women's equality or advocating for the rights of women, at least in theory, but they felt that the word *feminism* should not be claimed by the church. In fact, when I called myself a "Christian feminist," they just came short of calling me blasphemous. One guy was literally like, "I don't think you should ever call yourself that again."

As much as I would like to get heated right now and get on my soapbox about how the church and society have treated women over the years, that is not the point of this book or this chapter. As you could probably tell by now, the goal of this book is to get us all to think differently, to push past our current conceptions and understandings in order to think about what is truly important. The fact of the matter is, if we are getting into a verbal judo match over whether the word *feminism* should be a part of Christian vocabulary, then we are missing the point. This is something the Pharisees would be all over, holding conventions and tribunals over the issue of one word. Meanwhile, the needs of women both inside and outside the church would be woefully neglected, the gospel would not be proclaimed, and everyone would be caught up in semantics rather than professing the love of Christ in both word and action.

The reality is, especially in the past one hundred years, a lot has changed for women in America: securing the right to vote, becoming a larger portion of the workforce, having greater access to educational opportunities, securing victories against sexual assault, harassment, and domestic abuse, and so on. When you think about the rights and treatment of women across all human history, we have experienced rapid exponential growth in the past one hundred years. However, in a rapidly changing cultural context, it becomes increasingly more difficult to have to constantly reinterpret how the Bible relates to a given point in history. This process is complicated by the fact that each generation of believers has grown up in a vastly different cultural context. My experience as a Christian woman in America is vastly different from the experience of my mother and is not even comparable to the experience of my grandmother. And if I ever have a daughter, I am going to have to raise her up to be a godly woman in a new cultural context that may even seem foreign to me.

Therefore, even though I truly believe that the Bible was meant for all cultural contexts across all time and space, figuring out how to practically interpret the Bible in your everyday life in a rapidly changing cultural context is indeed a difficult task. As a result, it has become increasingly more challenging to disentangle societal expectations of women from biblical expectations of women. Scripture has frequently been utilized (often out of context) to justify cultural norms within and even outside of the church. However, when those cultural norms change, the church is forced to either quickly adapt or backpedal to stay congruent with the times.

Unfortunately, culture has often been the first mover when it comes to setting norms for women in society, challenging the church to either get with the times or look outdated or old-fashioned. As a result, the church is constantly on the defense, rather than taking initiative on setting an example for what it means to be a godly woman in today's society. Over time, this can lead to the impression that the church and scripture are inconsistent or contradictory in their views on women, leaving people even more confused or even cynical.

This, however, is not entirely the church's fault. Even when we look at the feminist movement, although the definition of feminism has remained the same over time, what it means to be a feminist from a practical standpoint looks dramatically different today than even ten or fifteen years ago. In fact, I can also pretty much guarantee that there are many feminists out there who would scoff at the idea of me calling myself a feminist because I do not share many of the progressive beliefs that are being perpetrated by the feminist community today.

The point in me saying all this is to highlight the fact that trying to perfectly reconcile cultural and biblical standards is a losing game, not because the Bible is no longer relevant or cannot be applied to different cultural contexts but because culture is constantly changing. It's like trying to shoot an arrow at a constantly moving target. And the more the church hyper-focuses on trying to hit the moving target, the more the church loses its perspective on the immovable target of righteousness, that is Jesus Christ.

Therefore, I could sit here and go through all the passages on women in the Bible to dissect the roles women should be playing in today's society; however, there are a lot of books out there on this topic, and to be honest, I think many of them have caused even more confusion or dissension. I also don't just want to speak to this particular point in history, because even five years from now, we could be wrestling with a whole different set of issues related to women. I could also make an argument for why Jesus was a feminist, but as previously discussed, our definitions of feminism have changed over time, and no one can really agree on what it actually means to be a feminist. Thus, I do not want to unintentionally put Jesus in a box made by humans.

Have you read them?

If you take a step back though and look at the big picture, there are two questions I think are the most important when it comes to gender and Christianity that no one is really talking about:

1. Are both men and women being fully equipped and empowered to proclaim the gospel and to be on mission for Christ?
2. Are our marriages and families a reflection of the gospel and fostering our sanctification by setting us apart and making us more like Christ?

These questions are not specific to a given point in history but are intended to make us think about the things that shouldn't change over time. Although I will examine these questions through the lens of what it looks like to be a Christian woman today, I believe that the heart behind these questions should transcend time and space.

At the end of the day, both men and women really have two main goals as believers: to share the love of Christ and to become more like Christ in the process. That means we should always be holding these two goals close to our heart as believers, using them as our compass to guide our thoughts and actions. When tricky and controversial questions arise, it is easy to stray from what, at the end of the day, is truly important. Therefore, I don't have the space to tackle all questions related to gender and Christianity in this chapter, but I want to discuss these two larger questions in more detail in hopes that they will shed light on some of the other questions we may have in the process.

Question 1: Are both men and women being fully equipped and empowered to proclaim the gospel and to be on mission for Christ?

I want you all to take a moment to imagine what it would have been like to be a part of the early church. This Jesus guy who claimed to be the Messiah was crucified and then rose from the dead three days later! You might have even seen Him in person during the forty days He was on earth before he ascended back into heaven. People were flipping out. Jesus was all people could talk about. Did you hear what happened? Did you see Jesus? Did you see the empty grave? Who is this guy? How can this be? How is this all possible?

The Bible says everyone was together during this time, meaning they had all congregated in one place to discuss everything that had happened. Everyone was trying to figure out what to do next. Their lives had literally been flipped upside down, and they were soaking it all in. It would have been surreal. *I can't believe this is all happening! My mind is blown! I never thought this day would come!*

Then, a few days later, during the Day of Pentecost, the Holy Spirit comes down from heaven like a violent wind that shakes the whole house. Everyone (men and women included) were filled with the Holy Spirit and were speaking in tongues and prophesying. This fulfilled the Old Testament prophecy in Joel that specifically says that the Holy Spirit would be poured out on all people and that men *and* women would prophesy (Joel 2:28–29). It is important to clarify here that in the Bible, prophesying was not about predicting the future, which is often what our modern-day conception of prophecy is. Instead, it was about speaking truth and revelation from God through the Holy Spirit to edify the larger Christian community.

Can you imagine how unbelievable the Day of Pentecost would have been? After Jesus ascended into heaven, everyone would have been wondering what was next. How can the ministry of Jesus be continued now that Jesus is no longer with us? Then *bam*! Enter the Holy Spirit. People were connected to God in a way they had never experienced before. God was speaking to them directly and was giving them divine insight into His plan for the world. On top of all that, they were all experiencing this at the same time. It was a collective experience. It wasn't as if a select few were having to relay their experience to the masses, trying to describe how cool the Holy Spirit was. They all got it. They all understood what everyone else was experiencing because they were experiencing it too.

Therefore, it is not a surprise that after receiving the Holy Spirit, members of the early church were filled with a sense of clarity and purpose. Acts 2 tells us that they sold all their possessions to give to anyone who had need; they were completely devoted to the apostles' teaching; they met together every day to eat together and have fellowship; they continued to praise God and worship Him. The apostles continued to heal and do miracles, and people were becoming new believers by the thousands.

It would be an understatement to say that their new normal was not even close to what they were used to prior to receiving the Holy Spirit. Things that used to matter to them, they couldn't care less about. They weren't worried about their jobs, their finances, their homes, their health, their status, their old customs and norms. Members of the early church literally thought that Jesus would return in their lifetimes, and thus they were willing to give up everything for Christ. They were on a mission, and nothing was going to stand in their way. It was an all-hands-on-deck kind of situation, and everyone was stepping up to the plate.

It honestly sounds like an amazing time to be alive. The sense of community and shared purpose would have been exhilarating. It would have been so evident that God was alive and at work in the world. Everyone

Jew/Gentile divide? *Idealization.*

would have been constantly sharing what they were learning about God and how God was changing their lives. People were now connected in a way that no one could have even imagined. The Holy Spirit was a great equalizer, bringing people together from all different walks of life. Everyone had value because the Holy Spirit had value, and it was manifesting itself in both men and women alike.

Thus, it is no wonder that the early church exploded like it did. Christianity was contagious. Everyone wanted the joy and hope that the early Christians had. They wanted to be a part of the club. Early Christians truly viewed one another as one big family and treated one another as brothers and sisters. Everyone had value, and everyone's stories mattered because they brought even more glory to God.

Fast-forward two thousand plus years, and again, it is no wonder that Christianity (in America at least) is in decline. Like the Pharisees, we have become more preoccupied with who has the "authority" to "preach," rather than sharing the actual good news of Christ. We no longer view the mission of Christ as an all-hands-on-deck kind of situation. Sharing the good news of Christ has been relegated to a task for only pastors or missionaries. If you haven't gone to seminary, you are not "qualified" to teach about Christ. In fact, if you are just an "average" Christian, you can just sit back and let the "super" Christians do all the work.

As a result, we idolize our pastors and missionaries as these saintlike beings who have achieved some sort of spiritual superiority. Feeling inferior, we are reluctant to step up to the plate to offer up ourselves to the mission of Christ. And to be honest, for many people, this is a great cop-out. It is sometimes easier to hide behind our own inadequacies, rather than put ourselves out there and risk it all for Christ.

In fact, it is human nature to pass off our responsibilities so we can place the blame on others when things don't go according to plan, just like Adam immediately blamed Eve in the Garden of Eden when he was caught disobeying God's command. We can sit back and criticize the "church" for not doing its job, when in reality the church is made up of all believers, and only some of them are doing their part. It's like blaming the coach for losing the game, when more than half the players never even showed up. Christianity is a team sport, and we need all the players to contribute.

So, how does this all relate to gender in the church? If Christianity is a team sport, then we need to value the contribution that all players have the potential to offer. We can't afford to bench more than 50 percent of our players. And honestly, I am not even talking about whether women should preach in the church, because I think the issue is much bigger than that. The beauty of the early church was the fact that it was decentralized. It got rid of old authority systems put in place by the Pharisees. It was communal, and everyone was equally a part of the mission of Christ. The attitude of early Christians was one that said, "Here I am. How can I help? Where is the need? Send me."

One hundred percent of church members should be serving in ministry, but we don't even come close to achieving full participation. However, part of the problem is that our modern conception of *ministry* is viewed through the lens of official church *ministries* within the church. Women's ministry. Men's ministry. Children's ministry. Homeless ministry. Worship ministry. I am not saying that these aren't important institutions. They are run by awesome believers who are doing the good work of Christ.

However, these formalized ministries sometimes make it seem like you can only serve Christ in an official capacity. This then raises questions of what roles can be filled by whom? What ministries can women lead? What qualifications do you need to fill a particular role? How big should each team be? Which team should receive the most resources from the church? How many ministry teams can the church support in the first place? What positions are open and need to be filled?

When we start viewing ministry as an organization, we forget that ministry is a movement. The early church grew so quickly because everyone was on fire for God. Everyone was sharing the good news of Christ. Everyone was offering up what they had for those who were in need. The gospel transformed their whole life, not just parts of their life. People knew who the Christians were because their lives looked radically different from before, not just because they attended church once a week and served for a few hours a month in a church ministry. Christianity was popular because it abolished the hierarchy, not because it imposed new hierarchical systems and rules for people to follow. Christianity was for everyone, and everyone had the opportunity to be useful for Christ.

In the face of intense persecution and the fear of losing your life, semantics fall to the wayside. When faith is a life-or-death decision, you are forced to think about what is truly important. However, we don't face this type of persecution in the United States today. We have lost our sense of urgency. We are playing it safe.

There was a period in my life when I was really frustrated with the limitations I faced as a woman in the church. I believe that teaching and leadership are among some of my spiritual gifts, and I didn't know how I was going to be able to use those gifts as a woman in most American churches. It made me both cynical and critical. Why would God give women these gifts if they aren't allowed to use them?

However, it then hit me that there were no limitations to the ministry opportunities I could do outside of the church. I could still live 100 percent on mission for Christ as a woman and use all my spiritual gifts without anyone blinking an eye. I could lead businesses and departments, teach college classes, write books, mentor students, and engage with my community as a representative of Christ. I could share the gospel with my colleagues, my neighbors, my friends, and my classmates. I have never had a formal ministry role in the church (except for being a high school youth leader), but I honestly have never felt like I have been unable to utilize my spiritual gifts.

The irony was no one was criticizing me for teaching, preaching, leading, and prophesying outside of the church! More often than not, I have been praised for the ways I have lived out my faith in the world (regardless of my gender). This got me thinking. Maybe the issue isn't whether or not women should serve in leadership roles in the church, but whether our modern conceptions of an organized church truly are a reflection of what Jesus had in mind. I am not claiming to have a perfect solution for what the modern church should look like, but I feel confident in saying that the modern church today looks nothing like the early church. If anything, we look more like the hierarchical system of the synagogues created by the Pharisees than the decentralized early church where the Holy Spirit made everyone one in Christ.

In fact, the more I engaged in ministry opportunities outside of the church, the less interested I became in ministry opportunities within the church. Jesus says in Mark 2:17, "It is not the healthy who need a doctor, but the sick. I have not come to call the righteous, but sinners." Jesus could have spent His time and energy with anyone, but He chose to spend them with tax collectors, prostitutes, Samaritans, lepers, widows, and orphans. He did not come to reorganize the synagogues and create new hierarchical systems for the Pharisees. He came to tear down existing institutions, not create new ones.

Maybe if we shifted our attention to all the work that needs to be done, we would care less about who is the one doing it. We have been so preoccupied with the question of who can fill a handful of leadership positions within the church that we have neglected to commission the vast majority of church congregations to the important roles that God has prepared for them to fill. At the end of the day, all of us must account for how we utilized the time, talents, and resources that God gave us. And to be honest, if we are doing it right as a church, most of us should *not* be commissioned to leadership positions within the church. Granted, some people have to hold down the fort, but the most important work that needs to be done is outside the walls of the church.

Therefore, what if the position of a businesswoman or a teacher or a barista or a politician or a PTA president were regarded as highly as the position of a pastor? We all as individuals (both men and women) have platforms of influence that we are called to utilize as Christ's ambassadors. All of us should be examining the areas of our lives in which we can be a light in the darkness, and we should all be trying to reach just as many people as our local pastor is.

However, if we are to equip and empower both men and women to proclaim the gospel and to be on mission for Christ, we have to look at the messages that are being sent to both men and women in the church, and the reality is, in the words of Leah MarieAnn Klett, "the version of Christianity that for years has been presented to women is not the version marketed to men; it's characterized by inspirational messages and fluff. But women, just like men, are faced with all sorts of issues in life—and fluff isn't going to hold us."[51]

---

[51] Leah MarieAnn Klett "Women in the Church: How can churches better equip women to serve in leadership?" *The Christian Post*, February 24, 2019, https://www.christianpost.com/news/women-in-the-church-how-can-churches-better-equip-women-to-serve-in-leadership.html

When I was in college, I was involved in an on-campus ministry. Although I loved being a part of this ministry and am so thankful for the mentorship and growth I experienced during my time in college, I hated being involved in women's ministry. If I had to hear another fluffy message on "finding our identity in Christ" over crafts and painful icebreakers, I was going to lose my mind. Feeling convicted though, I decided that instead of being critical of women's ministry, I should get involved and start changing the culture from within, rather than chastising it from afar. As a result, I decided to join the planning committee for the annual women's retreat.

We were in the brainstorming phase of retreat planning, discussing different theme ideas, and I suggested that the theme that year should be called "Women Warriors," with the focus on equipping women to be on mission for Christ. At first, the women around me seemed to like the idea. It was a refreshing change of pace. It was empowering. I was starting to feel energized. The ideas kept flowing—and then one girl raised her hand and said that she thought the title "Women Warriors" was too masculine and would send the wrong message. She felt that it came across as too strong and that it wouldn't attract girls to attend. Instead, what if the focus of the retreat was on *finding our identity in Christ*? And just like that, everyone in the group had abandoned my idea and was on the identity in Christ bandwagon.

I literally wanted to bang my head against the wall. I almost walked out, but I exercised discernment and did not say what was going through my mind. It is not that I have an issue with the topic of finding your identity in Christ. In fact, that is an incredibly important topic that is fundamental to both men and women in their faith. In order to have a correct understanding of the gospel, we need to understand our new identities in Christ.

However, understanding our new identities in Christ is only step one. Once you fully understand your new identity, you are then called to action. Whether it is worshipping Christ, sharing the gospel, walking in our newfound freedom, taking care of the widows and orphans, or becoming a prayer warrior, understanding our identity in Christ should prompt us to have an active faith.

First Peter 2:9 states, "But you are a chosen people, a royal priesthood, a holy nation, God's special possession, *that you may declare the praises of him who called you out of darkness into his wonderful light.*" (emphasis added) We aren't just given a special identity so that we can feel good about ourselves. Our new identities have been given to us so that we may praise God and share with others how our lives have been transformed. Our identities require action.

The problem is, most of the time for women, the topic of our identities in Christ gets treated like a self-help sermon, focusing on how we can increase our self-esteem and abolish our insecurities. The focal point becomes ourselves, and as a result, we often become so preoccupied with ourselves that we miss the point. As much as we hate to admit it, it is our nature to dwell in our own sadness and shame. We even like to compete sometimes for who has it worse. Have you ever complained about your day only to have a friend try to one-up you by telling everyone why their day was much worse? We thrive off of self-pity and frankly love the attention.

However, I love this quote by Sharon Hodde Miller, "When the majority of messages for women are about our beauty and self-worth, we gradually get the idea that Jesus came to earth and died simply to help us like ourselves."[52] We begin to think that we cannot be on mission for Christ until we get past our own insecurities. Therefore, we spend a lifetime in self-help land, never fully advancing to our true mission and calling for Christ. In other words, being a *warrior* for Christ is a man's job, and women never get equipped to also be on mission for Christ because they are falsely taught that until they figure out their own issues, they can't be useful for Christ.

This is unfortunate because in Ephesians 6:10–13, it tells us all to "be strong in the Lord and in his mighty power. Put on the full armor of God, so that you can take your stand against the devil's schemes. For our struggle is not against flesh and blood, but against the rulers, against the authorities, against the powers of this dark world and against the spiritual forces of evil in the heavenly realms. Therefore, put on the full armor of

---

[52] Sharon Hodde Miller, "Women, Insecurity, and the Self-Help Gospel," *The Gospel Coalition,* October 4, 2017, https://www.thegospelcoalition.org/article/women-insecurity-and-the-self-help-gospel/

God, so that when the day of evil comes, you may be able to stand your ground, and after you have done everything, to stand."

Ephesians was written for *both* men and women. It does not just tell men to put on the full armor of God. This verse is inclusive of all believers. There is a spiritual war going on in the world, and we can't afford to have more than 50 percent of our army disarmed.

When Christ came down to this earth, He changed everything. We were all given new identities in Christ, and with our new identities, we were all given a new mission. With this new mission, we are supposed to share a new sense of unity that could not even be fathomed before Jesus arrived. Galatians 3:28 (ESV) says, "There is neither Jew nor Greek, there is neither slave nor free, there is no male and female, for you are all one in Christ Jesus."

When the world looks at us, it sees our various earthly identities: our gender, our race, our socioeconomic status, our nationality, our professions, and so on. When God looks at us, He sees one thing: His Son, Jesus Christ. Thus, our earthly identities fall to the wayside when we become followers of Christ, and the only thing that matters is how we are using our new spiritual identities to share the love of Christ and to advance His kingdom.

The first step in advancing the kingdom of God is to fully empower and equip both men and women to be on mission for Christ. It is the job of both men and women to share the gospel, and both men and women are called to be ambassadors for Christ in the communities that they are in. Men and women are both called to spend time in prayer and are both called to study *all* of God's Word.

We especially need to be doing a better job providing rigorous biblical teaching to both men and women in the church for the purpose of commissioning them out for the sake of the gospel. For example, when my husband and I lived in the Bay Area, we were really involved in an amazing church. On Wednesday nights, they offered an intensive Bible study for women in their twenties and thirties called Women of the Word (WOW). The goal of this ministry was to equip women with the Word of God so that they could be effective in the many different ministries (both inside and outside of the church) that they were a part of. WOW was a three-year commitment where you went through the entire Bible in those three years. You would read and study ten chapters a week on your own, and then on Wednesday nights, you would discuss those ten chapters in your small group, before listening to another woman teach on the upcoming ten chapters.

I unfortunately started the program a little late because of my class schedule in my PhD program, but the almost two years I was a part of this program were incredibly refreshing and life giving. I received true female mentorship from older women who volunteered as small group mentors, and I got to dig deep into the Word of God with my fellow sisters in Christ who had a hunger to know God more and to serve Him in all walks of life.

This Bible study was not just focused on a few female-related topics that women tend to struggle with but was designed to equip women with *all* of God's Word. It wasn't just focused on the parts of the Bible that specifically mention women but included all the teachings God gave to *both* men and women. How many times do women need to study Proverbs 31 before they realize there are thirty other proverbs that are also important?[53]

This is not to say that there aren't crucial differences between men and women and that there isn't purpose in ministering to men and women differently to address many of the issues that are perhaps more relevant for one group over the other. I am also not trying to say that we should ignore the tricky passages in scripture that do address men and women separately (although I do think that we should carefully examine the historical context under which many of these passages were written to gain better insight into their meaning). I truly believe that God made men and women differently for a purpose, and those differences should be celebrated, not diminished or demeaned.

However, I am trying to say that the overarching message of the Bible is the same for both men and women. A majority of scripture is not

---

[53] Small sidenote here, but Proverbs 31 was written by King Lemuel, who was transcribing the wisdom his mother gave to him. In other words, the audience of Proverbs 31 originally was a young man who was being taught by his mother what to look for in a mate. However, I have never seen a men's Bible study on Proverbs 31, that stresses the importance of looking for a woman who is of noble character, rather than focusing on superficial traits that will fade over time. Despite the fact that the main audience of Proverbs 31 was a man, somehow Proverbs 31 gets designated as the women's chapter, with a laundry list of expectations women must meet in order to find a husband. As a result, men often skip over Proverbs 31 because somehow they have come to believe that chapter doesn't apply to them

addressed to men or women specifically. In other words, when you look at scripture in its entirety, men and women have far more in common in terms of their spiritual identities and calling, and the tools God has given us (e.g., the Holy Spirit and God's Word) are also the same.

At the end of the day, we need our entire team to be as equipped as possible so that we can do the best that we can to advance the kingdom of God. Lies and deceit are Satan's playground, and he is looking for any weak spots that he can exploit to his advantage. As a result, he loves to cause dissention in the church so that he can distract us from the real mission of Christ. For years, he has had a stronghold when it comes to gender and the church. We have been so focused on what a woman's and man's *role* is in the church that we have forgotten that we all share a common identity and a common goal. We are all children of God, and we are all called to love God, serve others, and spread the good news of Jesus Christ.

As a result, we should all be striving to have the passion, unity, and urgency modeled by the early church. Our primary goal as believers (both men and women) should be sharing the love of Christ in whatever circumstances we find ourselves in. The work of a stay-at-home parent ministering to the families in their neighborhood is just as valuable as the work of a ministry team leader because the end goal is the same: to advance the kingdom of Christ.

Therefore, the church should not be like a dam, holding its members back safely behind its walls, with the pastor and ministry team leaders acting like the gatekeepers, letting only a little bit of water out at a time. Instead, the church should be like a flood that permeates all aspects of life and reaches even the most secluded corners. When we truly recognize the power of the Holy Spirit and that the Holy Spirit is in all believers, we are excited to see what God can do when the full body of Christ is unleashed.

Question 2: Are our marriages and families a reflection of the gospel and fostering our sanctification by setting us apart and making us more like Christ?

For years, I tried to figure out what it looks like to be a Christian woman in the twenty-first century. When I first entered college, I was fiercely independent and had big plans for my life and career. I had been a straight-A student my whole life and felt an immense amount of pressure (albeit self-imposed) to not let my intellect and education go to waste. I knew I wanted to go to grad school and had dreams of living and working overseas as either a human rights lawyer, an ambassador, or a director of an international nonprofit. My heart broke for the world and knew that God had work that needed to be done, and I was ready to answer the call. My dad has always called me a force of nature, because whenever I created a plan to do something, nothing could get in my way.

Enter in my now husband. When I was a sophomore in college, I met this cute Christian guy who I almost immediately had chemistry with. I was planning on going on a missions trip with CRU that summer to El Salvador, but the trip was going to get cancelled unless more guys signed up. One day, I overheard this guy talking in the student union about how he was thinking of signing up to do a missions trip that summer with CRU, and without blinking an eye, I marched right up to him and inserted myself into the conversation to tell him that he should go to El Salvador because we needed more guys. I proceeded to give him my number because the leaders of the trip were speaking that night at CRU and he needed a ride (neither of us had cars at this point in college, but I had a friend who had extra room in their car). That night, we totally hit it off, and we continued hanging out together, both of us convinced that the other was in love with us, while not wanting to admit that we too had feelings for the other. We started dating shortly thereafter.

I knew pretty quickly that this guy (Jonathan) was special. He was unlike any guy I had ever dated. He took his faith just as seriously as I did and was one of the wisest and kindest people I had ever met. I knew pretty quickly that I could marry this guy, but that thought scared me. I had always envisioned myself as this high-powered career woman who wouldn't get married until she was at least twenty-eight (in retrospect, such an arbitrary age). I honestly remember asking God one day why He had me meet Jonathan now. Why couldn't we have met five to seven years from now when I had fully launched my career and was a little bit more ready to settle down?

Although my husband has always been incredibly supportive of all my dreams and goals (which is one of the main reasons I fell in love with him), I couldn't quite reconcile in my mind how I was going to juggle it all. How was I going to be a wife and one day a mom while also being a high-powered career woman and traveling the world to share the good news of Christ? I was also struggling with questions of submission. It was not in my nature to be submissive, so was I even suited to be a godly wife?

At the end of the day, love conquered all my fears, and I realized that even though I couldn't imagine how I was going to juggle it all, I couldn't imagine living my life without my husband even more. Jonathan and I had many conversations about what our life would look like as husband and wife, but at the end of the day, we trusted that God would reveal to us what a godly marriage should look like, and we both desired to be obedient to Christ above all else.

Once we were married, I realized pretty quickly why God had me meet Jonathan at such a young age. Like iron sharpening iron (Proverbs 27:17), my husband and I were helping each other become more like Christ. I realized that many of the goals I had for myself were rooted in my own pride, as I desired to be admired and perceived as successful by my peers. I desperately wanted to be in control and had a difficult time trusting God and letting Him take the reins. My identity was often rooted more in my accomplishments than in Christ. I was impatient and was often secretly critical of others for being incompetent. Empathy has always been a struggle for me, and I have a hard time slowing down my pace to truly serve others.

My husband, on the other hand, is the opposite. He has the spiritual gift of faith and trusts God completely in everything. He is always quick to notice the people who are left out or who are feeling downtrodden and will go out of his way to make them feel included and loved. He is one of the most content people I know and is not motivated by climbing earthly ladders of success. He is incredibly patient and is always one to give people grace and the benefit of the doubt.

In being married to Jonathan, I not only became more cognizant of the areas of my life that needed some work, but also my desires changed as I was being challenged to be more like Christ. Similarly, there have been many areas that my husband has struggled in, and he would be the first to admit that I have also helped him change some areas of his life in order to also become more like Christ.

Moreover, the original vision I had for myself as a woman was a confusing mix of what the Bible taught and what the world said. I was so preoccupied with what my role would be in marriage that I was forgetting what the purpose of marriage was in the first place: to bring us closer to Jesus and to make us more like Christ.

Today, I am a professor and a writer. I am also a mom who works part-time from home to spend time with her babies. My husband is an engineer and the primary breadwinner in our family and has always brought in more money than I have, except the time when the company he worked for fell apart, and then for a short period of time, I was the primary — ? breadwinner. At different times in different seasons, we have had to take on different roles, but our calling as husband and wife has never changed.

Everything that we do or do not do has been driven by our desire to glorify God and to be more like Christ. We don't view our jobs as our jobs; we view them as our mission field. We view our incomes through the lens of how we can bless and serve others. We are both actively engaged in the parenting of our children because we are both invested in raising our children up to be disciples for Christ. We study God's Word together and serve in ministry together because we know God is strengthening our marriage in the process. We both ask to be held accountable by the other because we know that we cannot do this on our own. We pray together every night because we both desire Christ to be at the forefront of our lives and our marriage.

The world teaches that you should not give up who you are for a man (or a woman for that matter). The church sometimes falsely teaches that a woman's identity should be subject to her husband. Both, however, are false doctrine. We should be 100 percent ready to give up our identities but only for Christ, and Christ alone. A marriage is a beautiful thing when both husband and wife have traded in their earthly identities for their new identity in Christ. There is a unity there that cannot be broken because it is held together by God. *A cord of three strands is not easily broken* (Ecclesiastes 4:12).

My husband and I have been married for over six years. I don't want to claim to be an expert on marriage, but here is one of the major things that I have learned so far. There has never been a time in our marriage in which God called my husband to do one thing but then told me something completely different. Sure, there have been times when we have been in disagreement, but when we humble ourselves, submit our differences to the Lord, spend time in prayer, and remind ourselves that our goal is to serve the other, we inevitably end up on the same page. God designed a husband and wife to be in perfect communion with each other. The Bible says that in marriage, the two will become one flesh. God is not in the business of causing divisions within a household; He seeks to foster unity.

Growing up, I used to hate reading the passage in Ephesians that tells wives to "submit" to their husbands. I was a strong, independent woman, and I wasn't going to let any man tell me what to do. However, before it tells wives to submit to their husbands, it first and foremost says, "Submit to one another out of reverence for Christ." This verse so often gets skipped over, but I believe it to be the most crucial part! Why do we submit in the first place? Because we seek to humble ourselves before the Lord and each other.

For those of you who are married or have been in a relationship, how easy is it to point the finger at your significant other and play the blame game when you are disagreeing? I have found, though, that when my husband and I start by humbling ourselves and owning up to our mistakes and sinful natures, we can turn a potential argument into a moment that brings glory to God and strengthens our relationship in the process, because we are submitting to each other out of reverence for Christ.

I think that the issue for many people is that biblical submission requires you to first submit to Christ, then to each other. If you are both submitting to Christ in the first place, you realize that your wills and desires are the same as husband and wife, not because one person had to bend the knee to the other but because your wills and desires reflect those of your heavenly Father. When one person is not submitting to Christ first, that is when issues start to arise. When an individual refuses to humble themselves and lay down their selfish desires, marital strife will inevitably occur.

I had a Bible study leader in college who told us girls once that it isn't hard to submit to a man who was submitting to Christ, and I have found that to be so true in marriage. When I see my husband in prayer, fasting over big decisions, being proactive about pursuing righteousness, repenting of his sins, asking for forgiveness, seeking wise counsel, and practicing humility, I trust him completely. I would follow him anywhere because I know that he is following God. However, if he is not doing those things and I am forced to decide whether to follow God or my husband, you better believe that I am picking God every time. My husband and I constantly tell each other that our goal in marriage is to try to out-serve the other. When my husband lays down his wants and desires for me and our family, I desire to do the same, and vice versa. The desire to serve one another should be contagious.

The problem is we live in a fallen world where many marriages are not built on the Lord, where both men and women put their selfish desires and needs above their spouse, where people are more concerned with being right than being righteous, where people would prefer to be first than last, where people are preoccupied with getting what they deserve rather than asking how they can better serve others, where both men and women want to be submitted to rather than wanting to submit to the other.

I don't think that people would have an issue with the concept of biblical submission within marriage if people were doing it correctly. Unfortunately, however, marital submission has been modeled poorly for most people, causing many to avoid the issue altogether. For many people, they have grown up in a household where one parent dominated the house, abusing their position of power to exert their will on their families. In these households, submission was a product of fear and insecurity rather than of love and self-sacrifice. Submission was one-sided and was never a choice but an expectation.

And yet when we look at the perfect example of submission given to us through the life and death of Jesus Christ, we see an entirely different picture. Jesus wasn't forced to lay down His life for us; He chose to lay down His life for us. He denied His rights, His comfort, His authority, His position of power, and even His superiority for the sake of love. He wasn't concerned with what was fair, or equal, or deserved. He gave himself up completely, even before we had an opportunity to respond. He gave His life up for us, knowing that many of us would not reciprocate.

If we truly desire to be like Christ in our marriages and families, we should be willing to do the same. We should be first movers when it comes to trying to serve our spouses and families, not because we are trying to get something in return but because we know that it is fostering our own sanctification. When both husband and wife are striving to be more like Christ, there is no longer a power struggle, because each spouse is trying to put the other first. It's like two teenagers in love who can't hang up the phone. *No, you hang up first. No, you hang up first.* Except, instead of debating who hangs up first, you are debating who gets to be served. *No, let me serve you first. No, let me serve you first.* We so often view submission as a chore rather than an opportunity, as something we have to do instead of something we get to do.

There are so many times in scripture where we are given a picture of what life <u>should</u> be, even though our current realities are far from that picture. The difficulty is not letting the world harden us so much that we give up on what life/marriage/relationships/community/church <u>should</u> look like. Even though your marriage will inevitably fall short of the ideal, that doesn't mean you <u>should</u> give up trying.

I don't know if you have ever scrolled through Pinterest fails on the internet. I find them to be absolutely hilarious and have had my fair share of Pinterest fails. I still remember these penguin cookies that my friend and I tried to recreate a few years back. The photos on Pinterest looked so cute, but ours seriously looked like creepy, misshapen ghosts.

Now if you were to continue to see people try to recreate this penguin cookie recipe and fail, you would be tempted to throw the recipe out completely. See? This recipe is dumb! No one can seem to do it correctly! It must be a sham. There is no way that someone actually made these penguin cookies that we see in the photos on Pinterest. They are probably just fake photos. It would be easy to assume there was something wrong with the recipe, rather than your baking skills.

However, what if you knew that this penguin cookie recipe was from a famous cook? What if Chrissy Teigen or Joanna Gaines was the one sharing their recipe for these adorable penguin cookies on their Insta Stories? Instead of thinking the recipe was a sham, you might instead think that maybe your penguin cookie baking skills were inadequate and that you probably needed a few practice runs before you could get it right. It would be extremely evident that Chrissy Teigen's or Joanna Gaines's baking skills were just far superior to the baking skills of most people out there.

We have seen so many marriages fail and have seen biblical submission in the context of marriage be so poorly done that it would be easy to assume that God's recipe for marriage was a sham and give up on it completely.

However, what if we instead recognized that maybe we, as sinful human beings, are just bad at marriage and are going to fall short of the ideal?

Are my husband and I in perfect submission to Christ and each other all the time? Of course not! I would like to say yes, but that isn't true. There are days when I think I know best and I want to undermine my husband to exert my own will. I am often impatient and controlling and want things to be done my way. There are other days when my husband is being selfish and forgets to lay down his life and his desires for me and our family. He stops being intentional and makes decisions based on how he feels in the moment. Sometimes we are both disciplined in prayer and reading God's Word, and other times one or both of us are more distant or stagnant in our faiths. Sometimes we ask God for His wisdom and discernment before making a big decision, and sometimes we forget and have to later ask for forgiveness.

In all our shortcomings, however, the goal is still to submit to Christ first and then to each other. The important part is that we share this goal. We both desire to have a righteous marriage. Biblical submission in the context of marriage is hard enough as it is, but it is even more difficult if one or both people do not share this goal. That is why the Bible warns us of the dangers of being unequally yoked (2 Corinthians 6:14 ESV).

At the end of the day, the purpose of marriage is for our own sanctification (to make us more like Christ). And when we look to Christ as our example, we see someone who laid down all His rights and His life for the sake of love. He desired to serve, not to be served. He put himself last instead of first. Becoming more like Christ is not glamorous. It is hard work and requires self-sacrifice. But if our desire is truly to be more like Jesus, then we should *all* (both men and women) be jumping at the opportunity to serve our spouses and families like Christ.

CHAPTER 11
LET'S TALK ABOUT SEX, BABY!

Shame no longer has a place to hide
And I am not a captive to the lies
I'm not afraid to leave my past behind
Oh, I won't be shaken, no, I won't be shaken
My fear doesn't stand a chance
When I stand in Your love

—"Stand in Your Love" by Bethel Music and Josh Baldwin

The church does not like to talk about sex. It is uncomfortable. People start squirming in their seats. No one wants to talk about their own sexual behaviors out of fear that they might be judged. Some experience high levels of guilt and shame. Others feel a sense of moral superiority. Therefore, it is easiest to avoid the topic all together. If we don't talk about it, we don't have to think about it, and people can just go about their lives making decisions about their own sexual purity that makes sense for them.

My husband and I were involved in high school ministry at church for about three years, and most of our students could tell us that sex before marriage was bad, but they couldn't explain why. Deep down, they wanted to know more, like how far was too far? What if you had done stuff already? Would God still love you? What about things like masturbation or porn? What about homosexuality? What does God say about that?

For most students, these questions go unanswered. Although they receive the message loud and clear that sex is bad, no one wants to take responsibility for walking through all the tough questions high schoolers have about sex. Then these students go off to college, and everyone seems to be *doing it,* literally speaking here, and they start to wonder, *Could sex really be that bad?* In fact, according to WebMD, by age twenty, 75 percent of people have had premarital sex, and by age forty-four, 95 percent of people have had premarital sex.[54] With statistics like these, chances are the people who preached at them to stay abstinent all these years probably had premarital sex themselves. Enter in feelings of resentment toward the hypocritical mentors in their life who really weren't modeling the behavior they were advocating.

Moving forward, these students then move on to their mid to late twenties and thirties when they are faced with decisions about whether they want to get married and have kids. They don't want to get divorced, as many of them, approximately 37 percent according to the PEW Research Center, grew up in households in which their parents were not together.[55] Many of them experienced firsthand how damaging divorce could be to families, relationships, finances, and stability. In a world in which almost 50 percent of marriages fail, why would anyone want to take the plunge?

As a result, these young adults delay marriage, experiment with cohabitation, and focus on their careers and own personal financial security, knowing that relying on someone else is a risky strategy. Meanwhile, the church relentlessly pursues its message of abstinence, knowing that a majority of its congregation is ignoring or has ignored their sexual purity battle cry. Over time, people then become tired of feeling guilty every time sex gets brought up. They don't want to have to continue to justify to their parents or church community why they are living or sleeping with their significant other without having said their marriage vows. As a result, these individuals start to taper off in their church attendance because it

---

[54] Jennifer Warner, "Premarital Sex the Norm in America," *WebMD,* December 20, 2006, https://www.webmd.com/sex-relationships/news/20061220/premarital-sex-the-norm-in-america#:~:text=Premarital%20Sex%20Research,-In%20the%20study&text=By%20age%2020%2C%2077%25%20of,sex%20had%20had%20premarital%20sex.

[55] Wendy Wang and Paul Taylor, "Comparing Millennials with Gen Xers," *Pew Research Center,* March 9, 2011, https://www.pewsocialtrends.org/2011/03/09/ii-comparing-millennials-with-gen-xers/

is easier that way. They might proclaim that they have larger issues with the church in general and that they can serve God on their own and don't need church to be a Christian, and there will be enough people who agree with them to make them feel justified.

I don't have data to back this up, but I would not be surprised if next to politics, sex is one of the biggest issues keeping people out of the church today, although no one would admit that. No one wants to say that they left the church because their sexual practices don't align with church doctrine. That would be getting too personal and would be admitting too much. No one wants to have that awkward conversation.

Now before I go any further, I think it is important for me to get personal here. My husband and I are actually in the small 5 percent of people who waited to have sex until marriage. When we met as sophomores in college, we both had purity rings that we had both been wearing since high school. When we started dating, early on we had conversations about wanting to save ourselves for marriage, and we set boundaries for ourselves to protect our sexual purity. After three and a half years of dating, we finally got married, and as we drove away that night in a rented red convertible Mustang, with Marvin Gaye's "Let's Get It On" blaring in the background, my husband and I actually got extremely nervous because we knew that we were both about to have sex for the first time.

I don't say all this to brag about how holy my husband and I were, or to make anyone feel guilty about their own personal stories. Waiting for marriage to have sex was one of the hardest things we had to do. Fighting for purity felt like an uphill battle. We would set boundaries, inch too close to them, put a toe across them, and have to restart and create a new set of boundaries. For most of our relationship, we were cautious about things like staying up too late together or going over to each other's places when our roommates weren't around. But were we perfect? Of course not! Some seasons were easier than others. Sometimes we couldn't keep our hands off of each other and had to get really strict with our boundaries, implementing no kissing rules that of course wouldn't last long. We both had accountability partners that we would confess to if we had broken one of our boundaries. We would often have to ask God for forgiveness when things got carried away and we were not being diligent about protecting our purity. It was messy, but we fought for our values and our convictions.

Now I am guessing that many of you are reading this and thinking, *Wow, that sounds like a lot of work. They probably were too legalistic and needed to cut themselves some slack. Good for them for making it until marriage, but it is unrealistic to expect others to do the same. They were young and naïve, and what worked for them doesn't translate well for different people in different circumstances.*

The point in me telling you all this is not to prescribe a certain set of decisions and guidelines for you all to follow. This isn't my how-to essay on saving yourself for marriage. I do, however, want to share with you what our experience in saving ourselves for marriage taught me about following Christ.

To this day, I am proud of my husband and myself for saving ourselves for marriage, not because it is a box that we get to check as a Christian married couple but because the experience of fighting for purity together, early on in our relationship, is symbolic of a larger attitude we have on marriage and following Christ. It set us on a path of striving for holiness in our marriage and in all aspects of our lives. In our dating relationship, we were given the opportunity to start developing habits that would sustain us for many years to come. Fighting for purity was just one challenge in a series of many to come that my husband and I would have the chance to put Christ first.

When my husband got laid off from his job in our first year of marriage, we immediately turned to Christ together for our hope, strengthening our marriage in the process. When we had to do long distance for a period of several months shortly afterward, our marriage was not shaken because we had built our marriage on a firm foundation in Christ. When I went through a season of battling anxiety and depression, we spoke God's truth into our lives instead of letting the enemy take ahold of our thoughts. When we moved to a new city and didn't have very much community, we took steps together to get involved in ministry and fellowship at our new church. When we were stressed about finances because I was on a grad student salary and we were living in the Bay Area, we thanked the Lord for teaching us to rely on Him and helping us to focus on building up our heavenly treasures rather than our earthly ones. When we found out we were pregnant, our first reaction was to start praying over our son, asking God to help us raise him to be a man of God.

A huge part of being a Christian is a series of decisions in which you are asked to put Christ first, even if it is not easy, convenient, or the cultural norm. When the world zigs, you sometimes have to be willing to zag. There may be times when your decisions seem weird, extreme, silly, naive, or old-fashioned to the people around you, but we are called to a higher standard that the world will never fully understand. We are not judged by the world's standards of morality but by God's standards of holiness.

Therefore, let me ask you a few questions. Are you willing to fight for the purity and sanctity of your marriage and family? Are you willing to go the extra mile to ensure that Christ stays at the center of your marriage and family? Are you willing to make earthly sacrifices in pursuit of holiness? Are you willing to deny yourself and your own desires for a larger goal or purpose? Are you and your spouse willing and able to make difficult choices together to maintain your values? Are you willing to go against cultural norms because you wholeheartedly believe that God's plan for creation is better than anything the world has to offer?

The issue of premarital sex is not a legalistic issue of what you can or cannot do sexually inside and outside marriage. It is a heart issue. If you are asking yourself what is or is not on the list of sexually appropriate actions, you are asking the wrong question. I used to tell my high schoolers that I wanted them to keep themselves pure and to refrain from having sex before marriage, but much more than that, I wanted them to *want* to be pure and to strive for a blameless and holy marriage. I wanted them to love God so much that they were asking God how they could glorify Him through their relationships, rather than asking God what they could get away with or how much was too much. I wanted them to be all-in Christians, not bare minimum Christians.

We are called as Christians to be holy, to be set apart, to look different than the rest of the world, in our marriages, in our relationships, and in our lifestyle choices. If our lives don't look any different than the lives of nonbelievers, then what is the point of being a Christian? We either believe that God changes everything or that God changes nothing. God is either at the center of our marriages, or He is not in them at all.

What no one wants to say about premarital sex is that really it is an issue of obedience. Throughout my lifetime as a Christian, I have heard many reasons for why we should wait to have sex until marriage. *God will bless your sex life if you wait. You don't want to bring any sexual baggage into your relationship. You don't want to struggle with comparison when it comes to having sex with your husband. Couples who have premarital sex are more likely to get divorced. Your wedding night will be more special if you wait. You and your husband will share a bond that you don't share with anyone else.*

Although there may be some element of truth in all these reasons for why you should wait until marriage, at the end of the day, however, none of these reasons really matter. Why did I save myself for marriage? Because I wanted to obey my heavenly Father and strive for righteousness and holiness in all areas of my life. Period. Any earthly blessings that come from my obedience are just an added bonus. Therefore, what if instead of focusing on what we *can't* do with our bodies as Christians, we focused on how we can use our bodies as a "living sacrifice, holy and pleasing to the Lord" (Romans 12:1). Our sex life, like everything else, is an opportunity to practice holiness. And when two people in a marriage relationship both desire to practice holiness above all else, that is a beautiful thing!

SHAME AND SEXUAL SIN

That all being said, I do think it is important to address the areas in which I think the church is messing up when it comes to sex, dating, and relationships. Somehow, somewhere, someone decided in the church that there was a hierarchy of sins, with sexual immorality being toward the top and homosexuality ranking even higher. Now the Bible does say in 1 Corinthians 6 that sexual immorality is different from other sins because it is a sin committed against our own bodies. However, here Paul isn't saying that sexual immorality is worse than other sins but that in addition to sexual immorality having moral and spiritual consequences, it also has physical ones. One only needs to look at STD and unwanted pregnancy statistics to know that this is obvious. In addition to these more obvious physical consequences of sexual immorality, research has also demonstrated that people who have multiple sex partners experience higher levels of anxiety, depression, and substance abuse.[56]

---

[56] Susan Krauss Whitbourne, "The Long-Term Psychological Effects of Multiple Sex Partners," *Psychology Today*, April 20, 2013, https://www.psychologytoday.com/us/blog/fulfillment-any-age/201304/the-lingering-psychological-effects-multiple-sex-partners

Thus, are there consequences for sexual immorality? Absolutely. Should we strive for purity and as 1 Corinthians 6:18 also states, "flee from sexual immorality," meaning we should be actively taking steps to not allow ourselves to be tempted with sexual sin? For sure. Should we be encouraging one another and holding each other accountable when it comes to sexual purity? Of course.

But should we treat individuals who have committed sexual sins any differently? Not at all. Should we be shaming people for their sexual sins and treating them like pariahs? I should hope not. Should we be teaching our children that there is a hierarchy of sins and only calling out the "really bad" ones rather than teaching them that we have all sinned and fallen short of the glory of God? No way!

By creating a hierarchy of sin and placing extra shame on some sins but not others, we are incentivized to compare our level of sin with others, rather than comparing our level of sin with Christ. We become obsessed with where we are at in the hierarchy, and as much as we hate to admit it, we can sometimes take pleasure in the fact that we aren't as bad as _____. *Thank goodness there are worse sinners than me, so I don't have to feel that bad about myself. Sure, I gossip and lie sometimes and get jealous, but thank God I am not like one of those real sinners who have premarital sex, commit adultery, practice homosexuality, or are addicted to porn.*

What if, instead, we had an attitude like Paul when he says in 1 Timothy 1:15–17, "Here is a trustworthy saying that deserves full acceptance: Christ Jesus came into the world to save sinners—*of whom I am the worst. But for that very reason I was shown mercy so that in me, the worst of sinners,* Christ Jesus might display his immense patience as an example for those who would believe in him and receive eternal life. Now to the King eternal, immortal, invisible, the only God, be honor and glory for ever and ever. Amen" (emphasis added).

We think of Paul as a spiritual giant, and yet here he is calling himself the worst of all sinners. What is more, he finishes by bringing the attention back to God, giving Him all honor and glory rather than honoring and glorifying himself. This is an attitude that reflects a correct view of ourselves in relation to God. When compared to Christ, who is perfect, we fall miserably short. We don't even come close. There can be no comparison.

I heard an analogy once that has stuck with me ever since. We are all comparing ourselves to one another on a scale from one to ten, arguing over whether we are a six or an eight or an 8.4. When comparing ourselves to Christ, however, the scale changes from one to ten to one to one billion. The difference between a six and an eight or an eight and an 8.4 is negligible when comparing these numbers to one billion. It seems silly to brag about ourselves being a point or two better than someone else when we are both basically a billion away from Christ. When comparing ourselves to a billion, we are basically a zero. We are all the worst of sinners when compared with the surpassing greatness of Jesus Christ.

Therefore, we need to stop shaming people when it comes to their sin, especially sexual sin! Shame is the playground of the enemy. It keeps people away from one another and away from Christ. It destroys relationships. It builds up barriers. It creates fear and tears down trust. Shame keeps sin hidden in the darkness rather than bringing it to the light. The more sexual sin is shamed by the church, the more sexual sin will remain ignored and unaddressed. Shame does not encourage people to speak up about what they are struggling with. Shame is adamantly opposed to forgiveness and grace. Shame is void of compassion. Shame is not from the Lord.

Conviction, on the other hand, is from the Lord. It is one thing to feel convicted by the Holy Spirit to repent and to make some changes in your life. It is another thing entirely to be wracked with guilt, fearful of bringing your sin to the light, isolating yourself from Christ and your fellow believers. The beauty of conviction is that at any point you can turn to God for His assistance when you have veered off course.

It's like playing the rainbow road track in Mario Kart, where every time you fall off the road (which for me is a lot), the little turtle guy in the cloud will always pick you up and put you back on the track. You get an unlimited number of do-overs. You just have to keep wanting to finish the race. You could, of course, at any time decide that the race is not for you and just give up, but who really wants to hang out in the black abyss?

I don't know where you are at in your own journey of sexual purity. You could be in the very small minority of people, like my husband and I, who waited (or are waiting) to have sex before marriage. However, just because you have made that decision doesn't mean that you did it for the right reasons. Others of you might have veered off the course when it comes to purity and are perhaps feeling convicted for your attitude toward purity. Some of you may have even given up on the battle for purity and are wondering if it is too late for someone like you. Has the damage already been done?

All I have to say here is that it is never too late to correct course. Purity is an attitude that can be changed at any time. It is a daily decision. Lamentations tells us that God's mercies never come to an end and are new every morning. You are not defined by your past decisions but the decisions that you make today. There is no barrier too big that God can't tear down, no sin too dirty that God can't wipe clean.

I love the verses in Romans 7:15–20 when Paul says, "I do not understand what I do. For what I want to do I do not do, but what I hate I do. And if I do what I do not want to do, I agree that the law is good. As it is, it is no longer I myself who do it, but it is sin living in me. For I know that good itself does not dwell in me, that is, in my sinful nature. For I have the desire to do what is good, but I cannot carry it out. For I do not do the good I want to do, but the evil I do not want to do—this I keep on doing. Now if I do what I do not want to do, it is no longer I who do it, but it is sin living in me that does it."

Each time my husband and I fell short of our goals for purity, I would think about this verse. This verse is not an excuse to keep on sinning, just because we can't help our sinful natures;it is a recognition that our desires are what matter. God judges our heart. He examines our intentions. Even King David, who was a murderer and adulterer, was called by God "a man after my own heart." This was because, despite the depth of King David's sin and depravity, he desired above all else to please God in his actions and attitude. The Psalms are full of instances in which King David is praising and worshipping God, humbling himself before the Lord, asking God to forgive him and to help him turn from his sinful nature, petitioning God to give him wisdom and purity, and acknowledging that he needs God's help (i.e., see Psalm 51). We will inevitably miss the mark and veer off course because we are human, but God looks to see whether we desire to get back on track. Do we desire His path for our lives above all else, even though we are prone to wander and get lost?

This is where I think a lot of people miss the point. At the end of the day, it is not necessarily about what we have or have not done. It is *also* about what we have or have not desired for our lives. Do we desire holiness and want to glorify God in *all* that we do, even though the battle might be tough and we might stumble along the way? Or do you desire the things of this world that will not satisfy and think that God's standards or purpose for our lives is a joke? Have you given up on the race before even giving it a shot? Sexual purity, like everything else, is an opportunity to practice holiness, to be set apart in this world, and to trust God's plan for our lives. It may not always be practical and it may look strange and legalistic to an outsider, but when our heart is truly set on following the Lord, purity should be a biproduct of our desire to become more like Christ.

CHAPTER 12
THE FALSE DICHOTOMY BETWEEN
SCIENCE AND RELIGION

I set every star into place
So you would remember my name
I made it all for you
You are my masterpiece
You are the reason I sing
This is my song for you

—"Dancing on the Waves" by We the Kingdom

I have been a college student for almost a decade (between my bachelor's, MBA, and PhD), and in the entirety of my experience in higher education, I have only had one professor who was openly a Christian (and not surprisingly, he was my Bible as Lit professor in undergrad). I had a few professors that I thought might be Christians, but they were never open about their religious beliefs. On the flip side, I have had a philosophy professor who openly chastised me for being a Christian in our class discussions, and a professor who gave me a C- on my public speaking final on abortion, simply because my "argument was not valid" (I had received As on every other speech up until that point).

Although I knew what I was getting into when I chose to enter into the public university system, I was always disappointed by the fact that there were so few believers in the field of academia and that the ones who were believers felt the need to stay under the radar about their religious beliefs. College is often the most formative time in a person's life, and when most of your college professors are not Christians, you start to wonder whether you can be smart and still be a Christian. What is more, college professors often have a lot more liberty when it comes to what they can say in the classroom, and as a result, many professors are incredibly open about their beliefs about the world. It is therefore not uncommon for college students at public universities to be exposed to a very secular point of view in their college classes.

One night, CRU, the college ministry I was a part of at Cal Poly, hosted a panel of Christian faculty members who were asked to speak about their experience as a Christian on campus. Not surprisingly, many of them discussed the fact that they were often a minority in their respective departments and were sometimes looked down upon by their colleagues for being a Christian. At the same time though, many of them also felt inspired to use their position to be a light in an incredibly dark place.

That night, after listening to these Christian faculty members speak, I decided I wanted to be a college professor. I always had toyed with the idea in the back of my mind, as I loved learning and wanted to teach and write; however, after that panel, I felt a strong urge to go on mission in the field of academia. I felt compelled to be a resource for Christian students who felt that they had no Christian role models in their department, and I felt called to be a representative of Christ in a field where Christians were becoming extinct.

I knew that it would not be easy. Getting a PhD is hard enough, let alone getting a tenure-track faculty job at a four-year university. Nevertheless, just like those who feel called to go on mission to Africa or the Middle East, I felt called to go on mission to the field of academia. Our higher education institutions are increasingly becoming dominated by nonbelievers, and Christians professors are increasingly becoming extinct.

According to a study done in *Sociology of Religion*, college professors are more than three times more likely to identify as atheists or agnostics than people in the general public (22.9 percent compared with 7.1 percent).[57]

---

[57] Neil Gross and Solon Simmons,"The Religiosity of American College and University Professors." *Sociology of Religion* 70 no.2 (Summer 2009): 101–129

The percentage of atheists or agnostics gets even higher (36.5 percent) when looking at professors at elite doctoral schools.[58] Conversely, 51 percent of college faculty say that they believe in God all or most of the time, but only 34.9 percent of college professors say that they are convinced that God exists.[59] Furthermore, only 18.6 percent of professors would describe themselves as a born-again Christian, and that percentage drops to only a mere 1 percent when it comes to professors at elite doctoral schools.[60] These statistics were also from approximately ten years ago, and so I would imagine that in line with larger societal trends, the number of atheist/ agnostic professors has only increased, while the number of Christian professors continues to decrease.

These statistics are mind-blowing when you think about the fact that the first universities in the US were Christian institutions (e.g., Harvard, Yale, Dartmouth, Princeton, etc.) and were designed to increase biblical literacy and to equip individuals to evangelize to others.[61] In 1881, 80 percent of universities were related to the church.[62] In contrast, as of 2001, only 20 percent of universities were religiously affiliated.[63]

Now, it is not necessarily the case that college professors are actively proselytizing a secular belief system, intentionally drawing students away from their religious beliefs, as many evangelicals would have you believe. Most students who leave the faith actually abandon their religious beliefs before they go to college, and for many students, college just represents a time in their life where their faith remains dormant.[64] It is also important to be honest with the fact that strict religious adherence is not necessarily conducive to the typical American college experience. Getting drunk at frat parties, sleeping around, and experimenting with drugs are typically

---

[58] Neil Gross and Solon Simmons, "The Religiosity of American College and University Professors."

[59] Neil Gross and Solon Simmons, "The Religiosity of American College and University Professors." 9

[60] Neil Gross and Solon Simmons, "The Religiosity of American College and University Professors." 9

[61] "Colleges And Universities With Religious Affiliations." *Encyclopedia.com* "https:// www.encyclopedia.com/education/encyclopedias-almanacs-transcripts-and-maps/ colleges-and-universities-religious-affiliations

[62] "Colleges And Universities With Religious Affiliations."

[63] "Colleges And Universities With Religious Affiliations."

[64] Daniel Cox, "College Professors Aren't Killing Religion," *FiveThirtyEight,* October 10, 2017, "https://fivethirtyeight.com/features/college-professors-arent-killing-religion/

frowned upon by the Christian community. In addition, waking up early and finding a ride to church can make it even more cumbersome for college students to engage in any sort of Christian community.

That being said, however, college is a time in which students are exposed to various worldviews. As a result, it can be a very confusing time for many students because their new role models and mentors may or may not share the same belief system or worldview that they grew up in. In addition, when some of the smartest, most well-educated people in their lives identify as being atheist or agnostic, it raises the question of whether knowledge (and science) are incompatible with religion and faith? In other words, can you still be smart and be a Christian? Or do you have to abandon your intellect and disregard the evidence unveiled by the scientific community to support your religious beliefs? Therefore, it is not a surprise that 66 percent of teenagers leave the church (for at least for a period of a year or more) in between the ages of eighteen and twenty-two,[65] and the number one stated reason for why young people left the church is because they "moved to college and stopped attending church."[66]

For young people in particular, I think that this science/religion dichotomy is a major stumbling block in their faith. Young people today are not only more educated than the generations before them, but they have also grown up in an education system that highly values the scientific method and focuses on knowledge that we can touch and see. As a nineties kid, I, like many of my millennial peers, was raised on Bill Nye the Science Guy, and I have such fond memories of watching his videos (on VHS of course) in my elementary school classes. We were taught in the words of Bill Nye himself that "Science Rules," and from an early age, we grew up thinking that science was something to be respected and that the scientific method was necessary for the advancement of knowledge.

However, as I got older, I realized that not everyone thinks that science rules. Particularly in Christian circles, science is often treated as completely antagonistic and incompatible with faith or religion. In fact, recent studies have shown that over time, Protestant identification and fundamentalist

---

[65] Griffin Paul Jackson, "The Top Reasons Young People Drop Out of Church," *Christianity Today,* January 15, 2019, https://www.christianitytoday.com/news/2019/january/church-drop-out-college-young-adults-hiatus-lifeway-survey.html

[66] Griffin Paul Jackson, "The Top Reasons Young People Drop Out of Church."

beliefs in the Bible are increasingly correlated to skepticism in science.[67] Furthermore, this skepticism is not just targeted toward anticreationism research but toward all scientific research, including things like climate change, medical research, and so on. Unfortunately, this can make Christians come across as naive, stubborn, or ignorant to the rest of the world.

On the other end of the spectrum though, you have many scientists, including good ole Bill Nye himself, who are actively engaged in trying to disprove biblical teachings. It is therefore no wonder that many Christians have become skeptical of science when there are actually scientists out there intentionally trying to attack Christianity through their research. It can also be incredibly frustrating and hypocritical because there are also many atheists and nonbelievers who revere scientific research but also conveniently choose to ignore or avoid any evidence that supports God, Jesus, or the Bible.

As a result, science and religion are often placed at opposite ends of some made-up spectrum. Have you ever heard someone say, "I don't believe in God. I believe in science."? It just kills me when I hear people say that because if you think about what people are actually saying, it sounds completely ridiculous. The definition of science is "the intellectual and practical activity encompassing the systematic study of the structure and behaviour of the physical and natural world through observation and experiment." In other words, science is a method, a way of doing things, a systematic approach, an activity. To say you believe in science is like saying you believe in double digit division; you believe that a method is useful for uncovering knowledge about the world.

To say you believe in God, on the other hand, is to say that you believe in a being or a person, not a method. The merits of a method are not diametrically opposed to the existence of a being. They are two different things. Science can be a useful method, *and* God can exist at the same time. Science might be an incredibly effective strategy of uncovering knowledge about the world, but science is not a belief system. Thus, putting science and religion on two ends of a spectrum is to create a false dichotomy that

---

[67] Darren E. Sherkat, "Religion, Politics, and Americans' Confidence in Science." *Politics and Religion* 10 no.1(March 2017): 137–160.

is incredibly confusing for most people. Contrary to popular belief, you do not have to choose between one or the other. You can believe in God and still find the scientific method to be a useful tool.

In fact, since the beginning of creation, God actually gave us the ability to learn about and discover the world. Adam was tasked with naming all the animals and thus became the world's first zoologist. He was placed in the Garden of Eden to work it and watch over it, making him the first botanist, ecologist, and environmental scientist. God designed humankind to be curious, to explore and discover, and to experience mastery over the world. We are by nature scientists.

SCIENCE CAN BE AN INCREDIBLE FORM OF WORSHIP IF CONDUCTED WITH THE RIGHT HEART POSTURE.

However, it is important to recognize that as much as humankind has uncovered about the mysteries of this world through science, what we don't know about the world still *far* exceeds what we do know about the world. Scientists have only explored and mapped less than 20 percent of the world's oceans.[68] Only 4 percent of the *visible* universe has been explored.[69] We only understand around 10 percent of how the human brain functions.[70] Of the estimated 8.7 million species on our planet, 86 percent are unknown.[71] We know only a tiny fraction of ancient history, and what we do know is pieced together from existing written records and archaeological finds that are limited and incomplete. As a social scientist, I can tell you that there are very few facts that we treat as law in our field, meaning that most of what we know is how much we don't really know; we live in a probabilistic world that continues to surprise us.

---

[68] "Ocean." *National Geographic Resource Library* https://www.nationalgeographic.org/encyclopedia/ocean/

[69] Clara Moskowitz, "What's 96 Percent of the Universe Made Of? Astronomers Don't Know," *Space.com*, May 12, 2011, https://www.worldwideboat.com/news/miscellaneous/ocean-vs-space

[70] Robynne Boyd, "Do People Only Use 10 Percent of Their Brains?" *Scientific American*, February 7, 2008, https://www.scientificamerican.com/article/do-people-only-use-10-percent-of-their-brains/

[71] Traci Watson, "86 Percent of Earth's Species Still Unknown?" *National Geographic*, August 25, 2011, https://www.nationalgeographic.com/news/2011/8/110824-earths-species-8-7-million-biology-planet-animals-science/

What is more, even what we do know is still hard to wrap our head around. For example, it is estimated that the mathematical probability of life existing on earth is one in 10^{450}, or by some models, 10^{600}.[72] In other words, it is mathematically impossible. In scientific circles, Earth has often been called the "Goldilocks Planet," because so many factors needed to be "just right" for life to be possible on earth. For example, if a planet is too close to the sun, it is too hot and liquid water boils into gas, but if it is too far away, it is too cold and liquid water freezes.[73] Earth is exactly the right distance away from the sun and has the right surface temperature to maintain liquid water, which is necessary for human life. It also has the right orbit that keeps it from falling into the sun or colliding with another planet.[74] If gravity was too high, we would all be crushed into the earth, but if it was too low, we would all start floating off into space. In addition, in order for life to be sustained on earth, earth needed to have the right amount of oxygen, carbon, and nitrogen, not too much radiation, enough light for photosynthesis, an adequate water supply, and so on.[75]

To this day, scientists have not found another Goldilocks Planet. Astrophysicist Erik Zackrisson from Uppsala University in Sweden recently conducted a study that found that there may be as many as 700 quintillion (a 7 followed by twenty zeros) planets in the universe but only one like Earth.[76] The closest we have come is a planet discovered by NASA, named Kepler-1649c, that is three hundred light-years from Earth and appears to have some potential.[77] It is a similar size to Earth and is in its star's

---

[72] Henry M. Morris, "Probability and Order Versus Evolution," *Institute of Creation Research,* July 1, 1979, https://www.icr.org/article/probability-order-versus-evolution/

[73] Caro Oliver and Aditya Chopra, "The Goldilocks planet: why Earth is our oasis," *Australian Academy of Science,* https://www.science.org.au/curious/space-time/goldilocks-planet

[74] Aatish Bhatia, "What Would Happen if the Earth Stopped In Its Orbit?" *Wired,* December 31, 2014, https://www.wired.com/2014/12/empzeal-earthfall/

[75] Christopher P. McKay, "Requirements and limits for life in the context of exoplanets," *Proceedings of the National Academy of Sciences of the United States of America* 11135(September 2014): 12628–12633.

[76] Nathaniel Scharping, "Earth May Be a 1-in-700-Quintillion Kind of Place," *Discover Magazine,* February 22, 2016, https://www.discovermagazine.com/the-sciences/earth-may-be-a-1-in-700-quintillion-kind-of-place

[77] "Earth-Size, Habitable Zone Planet Found Hidden in Early NASA Kepler Data," *NASA,* April 15, 2020, https://www.nasa.gov/press-release/earth-size-habitable-zone-planet-found-hidden-in-early-nasa-kepler-data

habitable zone, which means that the planet could support liquid water.[78] It also appears to receive a similar amount of light, which would mean that the planet's temperature could also be similar to Earth's.[79] However, Kepler-1649c orbits a red dwarf star, which according to NASA is "known for stellar flare-ups that may make a planet's environment challenging for any potential life,"[80] meaning that it has potential, but at the end of the day, we have no idea.

These numbers and scientific discoveries blow my mind! Although it is honestly impressive that we are able to make these types of calculations and that we have the technology that allows us to study some of the vast intricacies of the universe, what we do know about the universe only introduces an infinite number of new questions yet to be answered. Like what is up with the other 700 quintillion planets out there? I literally can't even wrap my head around that number. Why can't we find another Goldilocks Planet? Why is Earth so special? How many universes are there out there? Is there life on other planets? Are there people out in the universe wondering about us, just like we are wondering about them?

It's no wonder that the best alternative explanation to creation out there is the idea of a multiverse, which is defined as "a hypothetical group of multiple universes. Together, these universes comprise everything that exists: the entirety of space, time, matter, energy, information, and the physical laws and constants that describe them." In other words, every infinite combination of reality must exist in order for our present reality to exist. Not to be cheeky, but there may actually be a universe with an alien going by the name of Clark Kent who fights crime with his laser vision and flies around in his tights and a cape beating up bad guys. Or perhaps there is even a universe where a teenager gets bitten by a radioactive spider and now has Spidey senses and can climb on walls.[81] But in our universe, we don't know why Earth is so special, so there must be an infinite number of planets and universes so that Earth is equally unique as every other planet out there. In other words, anything is possible when everything is possible.

---

[78] "Earth-Size, Habitable Zone Planet Found Hidden in Early NASA Kepler Data." *NASA*

[79] "Earth-Size, Habitable Zone Planet Found Hidden in Early NASA Kepler Data." *NASA*

[80] "Earth-Size, Habitable Zone Planet Found Hidden in Early NASA Kepler Data." *NASA*

[81] A special shout-out to my husband, the comic book nerd in our household, who insisted that he include at least one superhero reference in my book.

Is your brain hurting yet? Don't worry. Mine is too. I am in no way a scientific expert, and I do not want to pretend that I understand all the scientific discoveries that have been made (even just in our lifetime). What I do understand, though, is that we are all desperately searching for the answers to life's biggest questions, and just like everything else in our life, it is far more comforting to stick to what we know and understand, rather than to venture out into the unknown. It is easier to focus on the <5 percent of knowledge that we do have and draw conclusions from that than focus on the >95 percent of knowledge we don't have.

In fact, each generation of scientists likes to believe that they are on the cutting edge of research and that they are moving the discipline exponentially further than the previous generation. However, there is always a new generation of scientists that can look back and scoff at previous generations of scientists for how ignorant they were. Indeed, we have come a long way from thinking the world was flat, but even fifty years from now, scientists are going to look back at us and laugh at our own ignorance.

Moral of the story, science is a beautiful tool that can help us understand the world, but you could spend your entire lifetime studying people, the world, and the universe and would only understand a tiny fraction of it. We are so proud of what we do know, but in reality, it has taken humanity thousands of years to finally understand a small percentage of all there is to know. How many more thousands of years will it take to understand even just a few percentage points more?

As an academic who will probably spend my entire lifetime working with college students, I have often wrestled with how we teach our students. We develop curriculum and syllabi based off of the knowledge previous academics have uncovered. In other words, we teach from what we know. I am not necessarily saying this is a bad strategy, but what we unintentionally teach our students in the process is that they only need to know and understand what we have already discovered and understood. As a result, most students come out of their schools and programs thinking that they have learned all that they need to know on a particular subject or topic. They falsely assume that their education is complete. They get a neatly packaged version of knowledge that is supposed to help them go out into the world and make complex decisions in the face of all kinds of uncertainty.

It is completely misleading. What students don't end up learning from their educational experience is how much we don't know about the world and how much uncertainty there is out there. They see their teachers as experts on a particular topic who have it all figured out and falsely believe that if they pursue enough education, they too can be experts as well. If they don't understand something, they assume that it is from their own personal ignorance or confusion, instead of thinking that maybe the issue is far more complex or uncertain than they were originally taught.

The reality is what we know and understand about the world is just the tip of the iceberg, and we have no idea how far down the iceberg goes. However, we like to teach students that icebergs are just what we can see above the surface. In the process, we become so proud of how much we do know about the tip of the iceberg that we begin to think we are iceberg experts. *Trust me, I know what I am talking about. I have been studying the tip of the iceberg for decades.* We then become fearful of people who want to talk about anything that goes on below the surface because we are afraid that what we thought we knew will be called into question and our expert status will be jeopardized. As academics, we have an incentive to protect our knowledge and research from critique and judgment.

My point in saying all this is to remind us all to check our hubris. As we uncover the great mysteries of this world, we stumble upon even more mysteries. God's creation is infinitely more complex than our human brains can ever comprehend, and it is absolutely amazing that no matter how many layers we peel back, there are still more layers! Through science, we can better understand how powerful and majestic our heavenly Father is. Science can be an incredible form of worship if conducted with the right heart posture.

For example, in Psalm 8:3–4 (ESV) it says, "When I look at your heavens, the work of your fingers, the moon and the stars, which you have set in place, what is man that you are mindful of him, and the son of man that you care for him?" In other words, the more I study all that You have created, the more humble I become. The fact that the Creator of the universe desires to be in relationship with us should bring us to our knees in worship. In fact, the more we learn about God's creation through science, the more in awe we should be.

I love this quote from C. S. Lewis's book *Screwtape Letters*. If you aren't familiar with the book, it is an allegory written in the form of letters from a demon named Screwtape to his protege, a younger demon named Wormwood. It is possibly one of the best books I have ever read, and if you haven't read it, I *highly* recommend it. Screwtape is instructing his apprentice, Wormwood, on how to corrupt his "patient," a young man who is coming back into his faith. In one of his letters, Screwtape writes, "Above all, do not attempt to use science (I mean, the real sciences) as a defence against Christianity. They will positively encourage him to think about realities he can't touch and see."[82]

The irony is that Christians are often fearful of science because they are afraid that it will call their faith into question and might prove that God doesn't exist. However, if God truly created the universe and gave humankind the ability to discover and exhibit mastery over the earth, then science should only amplify God's greatness, not undermine it. When scientific discoveries seem contrary to biblical teachings, it could mean that the science behind it was flawed, but it could also mean that we just don't have the full picture yet. We are uncovering pieces of the puzzle, but we don't know how they all go together yet.

Therefore, as Christians, we do not need to feel threatened by science. Science was not intended to be the antithesis to faith. Instead, I fully believe that science is meant to be complementary to faith. Knowing what you can understand and see gives you an appreciation for what you can't understand or see. No matter how you slice it, we do not and will not ever have all the answers. If God wanted us to have all the answers, He would have given them to us. God was and is perfectly capable of clarifying passages of scripture that may be confusing to us. He could totally give us the scientific ability to understand all creation. But if we had all the answers, we would not need faith. According to Hebrews 11:6, "Without faith it is impossible to please God, because anyone who comes to him must believe that he exists and that he rewards those who earnestly seek him." Our faith is credited to us as righteousness.

---

[82] C. S. Lewis, William Dendy, and R. B. Green, *The Screwtape letters*. (London: G. Bles, 1952)

Furthermore, Hebrews 11:1 (ESV) defines faith as "the assurance of things hoped for, the conviction of things not seen." We can spend our lifetime studying the world, but we will still only understand a fraction of it. Consequently, faith does not discredit what we do know and understand but allows us to not feel threatened by what we do not know or do not understand. It gives us hope and peace when things do not make sense or when things don't go as expected or planned.

As Christians, we are playing the long game here. It's like watching one of the thousands of detective shows that are out there. We have all watched enough of them to know that the ending will often surprise you, and you can't draw conclusions from the first couple of clues they find. We don't always see what the main detective sees, and we may not fully understand it all until the ending is revealed. However, that doesn't mean we can't try to figure it out along the way; it just means that we have to also recognize that we don't have the full picture either.

At the end of the day, can you still be smart and be a Christian? Can you respect scientific discovery without your faith wavering? Yes, and yes. In fact, I truly believe that we need more Christians in academic and scientific circles who are able to be role models for what it looks like to find joy in uncovering new things about the world while also demonstrating humility by recognizing how much there still is to learn. As Christians, we need to reclaim science as a form of worship.

In fact, Romans 1 tells us that we are without excuse. God's eternal power and divine nature have been woven into all creation and can be clearly seen by those who look upon creation with a humble heart. The problem is, as Romans 1 continues, we look upon creation and forget to honor and thank God, hardening our hearts and becoming prideful in our thinking. In doing so, we start worshipping creation rather than the Creator.

Ultimately, science can be a beautiful form of worship or a major stumbling block, depending on your heart posture toward the Lord. Therefore, blessed are those who are able to humbly weigh what they do know and what they do not know and correctly conclude that what they don't know is infinitely greater than what they do know. Then, understanding that what they do not know is far greater than what they do know, they are able to fully understand why faith is so crucial to our relationship with God. If we had all the answers, we would be God. But we clearly do not have all the answers; we are not God, and we need to have faith that one day all the mysteries of the world will make sense when God chooses to reveal them to us. In the meantime, however, we can explore the vast intricacies of God's creation to better cultivate a sense of wonder for the almighty God, our heavenly Father, Author of life, and Creator of the universe.

CHAPTER 13
USHERING IN A NEW GENERATION OF CHRISTIANITY

'Cause Your power and Your presence
Breaks strongholds, King of Heaven
When You speak, mountains move
I believe there will be breakthrough

—"Breakthrough" by Red Rocks Worship

We talk about all the changes we would like to see in the world, but at the end of the day, what we need first and foremost is a heart change.

We are angry and frustrated with a God we don't even know or understand.

We view things through the world's lens rather than through the eyes of God. We are focused on the here and now while forgetting about the big picture.

We parrot the wisdom of the world without examining how it stacks up against the ultimate wisdom of our heavenly Father.

We are critical of a book that we haven't even read.

We advocate for earthly solutions to eternal problems, forgetting that we are not citizens of this world but are ambassadors for our heavenly kingdom.

We like to criticize at a distance but are rarely willing to put in the hard work to create the necessary changes ourselves.

We are so eager to debate the semantics of an issue that we forget the heart of the issue.

We are so willing to sacrifice the reputation of Christ and our fellow believers for the sake of our own.

We put our faith in positions of earthly power, hoping to delegate the hard work of God's kingdom, instead of being the hands and feet of Jesus ourselves.

We confuse the American dream with our spiritual calling.

We prop up hierarchical systems, focusing on what we think we deserve rather than laying down our rights for the sake of the gospel.

We are beholden to political parties, artificially butchering up God's agenda into two diametrically competing sides.

We have accepted a watered-down version of Christianity that cherry-picks pieces of scripture to justify our actions and beliefs.

Overall, as Christians, we are missing the point.

But it doesn't have to be this way. We have the power to usher in a new generation of Christianity.

One that keeps the gospel at the center of all that it does.

One that relies on the guidance and direction of the Holy Spirit.

One that exercises discernment on when to speak but isn't afraid to stand up for biblical truth.

One that pursues social justice not just for social justice's sake but as a vessel for sharing the hope and good news of Jesus Christ.

One that celebrates human diversity because it is a beautiful reflection of our heavenly Father.

One that worships the Creator rather than creation.

One that is blameless and unashamed in a world that wants to place blame and shame.

One that is solely concerned with bringing God glory instead of pursuing glory for ourselves.

One that sees the value that all members of the body of Christ can contribute.

One that studies God's Word and has a desire to know Him more.

One that reaches across party lines to advocate for God's plan for creation, not some politician's or political party's plan.

One that is more concerned about being righteous than being right.

One that strives to be holy, to be set apart, to look different from the world.

And one that is giving people an insatiable taste of heaven here on earth.

A Final Note from the Author

In writing this book, my hope and prayer has been that our generation would witness a breakthrough when it comes to Christianity, that our current trajectory would not be sustained, but that we would correct course and create a new reputation for believers in the world today. I want our generation to be associated with the revival of Christianity, not the decay. Although we may be discouraged and overwhelmed by all the things we would like to see changed, we are not yet tapping into our full potential given to us by God through the power of the Holy Spirit. Sometimes we are our own worst enemies.

However, the purpose of this book is not to bring discouragement but to bring hope. I want to cast a vision of what it can look like to be followers of Christ today. Whereas some might say that being a Christian is a challenge right now, I see that challenge as an opportunity. We have the ability to surprise people, to open their eyes, and to change their minds. Let people expect the worst but get the best.

At the end of the day, the world will continue to disappoint us. Each generation of believers will have to wrestle with a new set of issues, face new challenges, reconcile their beliefs with new current events and trends, defend their faith against new adversaries, and combat new distractions designed by the enemy to pull us away from what is truly important. However, just like Peter when he was walking on water (Matthew 14), if we become distracted by the storm, we end up taking our eyes off Jesus in the process. The waves will continue to rage, the rains will continue to fall, but Jesus will always stay the same. Our feeble attempts at calming the storm ourselves will only result in us drowning in the process.

Therefore, each generation likes to think that they are special, that they face unprecedented times and unique challenges that are unlike the generations before them. However, the endgame has never and will never change. What is the point? Jesus is the point. When our eyes are fixed on Jesus, we no longer see the storm. We do not need to fear the wind and the waves, because our gaze is set on Christ. As a result, while the world is panicking, tearing one another apart, playing the blame game, and desperately clinging to earthly solutions to eternal problems, we should be a steadfast beacon of hope.

CPSIA information can be obtained
at www.ICGtesting.com
Printed in the USA
FSHW012031310821
84427FS